# GRISWOLD

## Volume 2

### A Price Guide

© 1994

**L-W BOOK SALES**

P.O. Box 69

Gas City, Indiana 46933

# TABLE OF CONTENTS

# INTRODUCTION

Griswold Cast Iron is one of the hottest items in the Antique and Collectible field today. Many collectors buy Griswold to decorate their homes, while others buy it to use for its original purpose.

Our first Griswold Book has been a great book. It is one of the Best Sellers on the Antique Book Market. Volume II was planned at the time the first volume was printed. We contacted many experts in the Griswold field and with their contributions, we compiled another book that should help the collectors and dealers tremendously. Without these experts we could not have done this second volume.

Griswold may be found anywhere from the country garage sale to the most prestigious Antique Shows. The prices will vary accordingly. We have used an "average" in determining a price for all items. This price will vary depending on the region that you live, etc.

# PRICING NOTE

*Please Note:* This is only a guide and L-W Book Sales cannot be responsible for any gains or losses incurred by the use of this book.

## Abbreviations

p/n = Pattern Numbers
TM  = Trademark

# ACKNOWLEDGEMENTS

A very special thank you goes out to the many collectors of Griswold who have so graciouly helped us put together a book for you on this very special hobby. All the pictures that were sent in were very nice. Thank you so much for sharing your special pieces with us.

We want to thank the following people who contributed greatly to this book. We appreciate it very much!

Joan Baldini of Erie , PA

Jay Brandt of Norman, OK

Christine Brown of Crystal Lake, IL

Nancy & Lee Brown of Pittstown, NJ

Frank D. Castle Sr. of Kenton, OH

Bill & Lynda Cervenka of Bunch, OK

Bob Chandler of Ridgeway, MO

Gene Corral of Roseville, CA

Larry D. Crawford of Alpha, IL

Linda deHaas of Ridgeway, MO

Daniel Demers of Rice Lake, WI

Rita Densham of Elyria, OH

Dave Diener of Hartford, WI

Larry & Sue Foxx of Carlisle, PA

William M. Gough of Florence, AL

John F. Hawkins of Eatonton, GA

Marlyn Helbel of Annapolis, MO

Thomas E. Jahnke of Springfield, OH

Ray & Kay Johnston of Sarasota, FL

David C. Lange of Erie, PA

Craig Leverenz of St. Paul, MN

Richard Miller of McConnellsburg, PA

Terry & Dana Miller of Klamath Falls, OR

Robert & Doris Mosier of Saegertown, PA

Linda Murray of Elyria, OH

Robert E. Nealy of Syracuse, NY

Joseph A. Noto, MD of Asheville, NC

Peter J. Pappas of Ferrisburgh, VT

Robert F. Petty of Fort Myers, FL

Charles R. Riley Jr. of Uncasville, CT

Kenneth D. Risley of Amarillo, TX

Sharon & William Roberts Jr. of McDonald, OH

Rex Rodgers of Republic, MO

CDR & Mrs. Frederick D. Smith of Accokeek, MD

Ric & Catherine Smith of Key West, FL

Carl G. Steele of Vero Beach, FL

Steve Stephens of San Anselmo, CA

Mr. & Mrs. Robert E. VanBuren of Cobleskill, NY

Gary & Charline Wineteer of Columbia, MO

By George T. Griswold
August 29, 1989

# HISTORY

The manufacture of the finest cast iron ware was established in the latter 19th century by two Erie, Pennsylvania, industrial families. The Selden & Griswold Manufacturing Company, predecessor to The Griswold Manufacturing Company, was founded in 1865 in Erie, Pennsylvania, and commenced operations in 1868 on the block at the northwest corner of Tenth and Chestnut Streets.

There were three co-founders of the Company: Samuel Selden, his brother John Card Selden, and Matthew Griswold, whose sister, Lydia Griswold, was married to John Card Selden. The Seldens were members of the leading industrial family in Erie County, and Matthew Griswold was a member of a distinguished pioneer Connecticut family which numbered three colonial governors of Connecticut among its members.

Matthew Griswold was born in Old Lyme, Connecticut, on June 6, 1833. He was the son of Matthew and Phoebe (Ely) Griswold. Matthew spent his first 30 years at home on the family farm in Old Lyme. In 1865, he moved to Erie and entered partnership with John Card (J.C.) and Samuel Selden.

John Card Selden, son of George and Elizabeth (Card) Selden was born in Erie, November 28, 1825. From 1844 to 1850 he worked in Troy, New York, where he was a clerk in a store. After several years in California, he returned to Erie in 1853 where he joined his father in the mercantile business, subsequently purchasing it from his father. In 1855, he married Lydia M. Griswold, a sister of Matthew Griswold who was destined to be his future business partner. John Card Selden died on May 12, 1898.

**SAMUEL SELDEN**

Samuel Selden was born in Erie on July 9, 1821. When he was a young man, he spent five years in Cuba as a financial agent for a sugar plantation and a large estate. He returned to Erie county where he worked with his brother-in-law, R.L. Perkins, who was at the time manufacturing paper at Manchester in Fairview Township, PA. Later he moved with his family to the city of Erie, and with Matthew Griswold, established the Selden & Griswold Manufacturing Company. He died on June 25, 1882.

The foundry was 100' by 150', and the plant also contained a finishing room about 30' by 90'. The building had two stories, an upper floor used for machinery and mounting room, a storeroom 30' by 40', and an engine and boiler room which contained an engine having 50 horsepower. The Selden & Griswold Manufacturing Company was the successor of the "Butt Factory" which had been started on the bank of the Erie Extension Canal west of Chestnut street. The earliest products included a separable door butt (hinge), the Company's specialty, and other articles of light hardware which included boiler accessories. There were approximately 20 employees.

The closing in 1871 of the Erie Extension Canal opened up the west side streets of Erie. Building succeeded building until the plant extended to Walnut Street. At this time, Selden & Griswold included items for restaurants in the line of wares. Examples would include long griddles and waffle irons large enough to produce six to eight waffles in one baking. The Company added kettles, dutch ovens, roasters, a gridiron, and a blank cartridge firing burglar alarm to the product list.

Around 1884, Matthew Griswold bought out the Seldens, and 100 men were employed on a full-time basis. Products included small castings, hollow ware of special sizes and extra finished ware, house furnishing utensils, and stove trimmings. In that year he manufactured and patented a cuspidor or spittoon on casters. The tobacco cutter was also introduced around this time.

The plant was severely damaged by fire on August 3, 1885, but it was repaired and remodeled that same year. The Griswold Manufacturing Company was chartered in 1897. Matthew's son Marvin, born November 18, 1868, joined the firm as treasurer.

About 1890 a young engineer, Arthur Vining Davis, from Pittsburgh Reduction Company, arrived in Erie with samples of a new metal called aluminum. He showed this to Matthew Griswold, hoping to develop uses for the new metal through casting; he found Mr. Griswold warm to the idea. When Matthew asked his secretary what a woman would want most in the kitchen to be lighter in weight, a tea kettle was her response.

**JOHN CARD SELDEN**

Since Pittsburgh Reduction Company was the only one at that time with smelting facilities for aluminum, it was agreed that Griswold would furnish a molder who would go to Pittsburgh with a mold for the tea kettle. Thus, in approximately 1893, the first aluminum cooking utensil was born. The company had become known as a manufacturer of the finest cast iron ware that could be purchased at the time, and now it was also the pioneer in the casting of aluminum. As a result, the company expanded further and became much more diversified.

In this same period, Matthew Griswold, true to his lineage, succumbed to the lure of politics, and commencing in 1890 was elected to two terms in Congress representing the Erie district. Charles A. Massing was hired in 1901 as a clerk. He was given the opportunity to become a salesman for the company and was associated in that capacity until his retirement.

In 1903 the Tenth Street plant was abandoned, and the firm moved into the "Shaw Piano Company" building on the corner of 12th and Raspberry Streets. The piano company had been established in March of 1890 and closed about 1903. Soon after, the Griswolds moved to their new site where numberous other buildings were added. By 1909, the plant occupied the entire square of Cascade, 12th, Raspberry, and the railroad tracks.

Matthew Griswold Sr. stepped down from his position as president in 1905, and his son, Matthew Jr., became president. Matthew Sr. remained chairman from 1907 until his death on May 19, 1919, and Matthew Jr. remained as president until 1913. Thereafter, the latter accepted a position with the General Electric Company as Erie Works manager. In 1914 Marvin E. Griswold became president of the firm and remained in that position until his untimely death at 59 in 1926.

The 1920s brought with it bustling business at the Griswold plant. During this time, about 1925, the Company began manufacturing a complete line of commercial cookware, and Matthew Griswold Sr.'s secretary, Etta Moses, was assigned broader duties. She became known as "Aunt Ellen" to millions of housewives who were sold on her advice about cooking tasty recipes with cast iron and aluminum. So well known was she that stacks of mail came across her desk every day asking for hints and advice. There was a cookbook by Aunt Ellen on the market for many years, "The Aunt Ellen Booklet on Waterless Cooking," copyright 1928, and recipes and instructions written by her were enclosed in the boxes with many of the cast iron and aluminum kitchen utensils. The company's products also included electrical appliances in addition to the wood, oil, gas, or coal stove top lines.

As transportation methods improved in the '20s, Griswold salesmen took the line nationwide. Busy routes included Erie, Maine, Florida, Washington, and California. One distributor from California purchased Griswold products by the full freight car and shipped and sold the quality Griswold ware overseas.

In 1927, Roger Wolcott Griswold, son of Matthew Sr. and Annie Brooks Griswold, was named president of the firm. Business continued to expand, but in the summer of 1937 there was a prolonged labor strike resulting from the refusal of company officials to recognize the CIO. After weeks of negotiations, in which city officials and police took an active part, employees went back to work. This was the first time in Erie's industrial history that labor made itself seriously felt in its demand for better working conditions and higher wages.

During World War II the company was active in producing products in support of the war effort. Most notable among these was a highly technological aluminum alloy casting which became the hub of the Hamilton-Standard variable pitch airplane propeller used on virtually all U.S. manufactured airplanes. Also produced in quantity was a small cast iron, finned projectile which could be fired at a target where it would explode like a hand grenade. During this period, output of cookware was maintained, but without the chromium and nickel finishes which had proved so successful during the prewar era.

In December 1944, Roger Wolcott Griswold, who had been president since 1927, died suddenly of a heart attack. His brother, Ely Griswold, assumed the presidency, and Roger W. Griswold Jr., who was plant manager, became vice president. Shortly thereafter, Ely Griswold, who was the controll-

**MATTHEW GRISWOLD**

ing stockholder, announced that the company was to be sold since he wished to retire. This engendered bitter lawsuits by two branches of the Griswold family who wished to block the sale. In the end, Ely Griswold prevailed, and the physical assets and the "Griswold" trademarks were sold in late 1946 to a syndicate of New York City investors. By 1947, all Griswold family members had left the company; Isador Tachna became president and manager with Abe S. Weissman as general manager and treasurer.

Thus ended the proud 81-year period since the founding of the company in 1865 by the Griswold family, and a period of corporate dismemberment and lowering of the quality of the company's products began. Soon to be gone were the fine, sharp iron castings with their precise, thin walls and smoothly ground and polished inside and outside finishes which characterized those produced under the earlier "Erie" and "Griswold" trademarks.

In 1948 finished ware was reintroduced, sales continued to increase, and complete cookware packages were introduced in the catalogues. The set included dutch ovens and skillets with hinged lids that could be used with either styles of cookware.

The Company participated in Erie's Bicentennial parade in 1951, and 2,000 small "Griswold Pup" paper weights (#30) were handed out to the crowd. Approximately 3,000 of the pups were made in all, 2,000 for the parade and 1,000 were a form of giveaway to large distributors.

As late as 1957, the company had advertised its line of commercial electric cooking products in various trade publications. Late in 1957, this line was sold to McGraw Edison Company, and on October 7, 1957, it was announced that the company's remaining iron and aluminum lines, along with the "Griswold" trademarks, had been sold to its strongest competitor, Wagner Manufacturing Company of Sidney, Ohio.

On December 7, 1957, the plant at 12th and Raspberry Streets in Erie, Pennsylvania, was closed with the remaining 67 employees losing their jobs. Thus ended The Griswold Manufacturing Company of Erie as a business and manufacturing entity.

This is the first building of the Selden & Griswold Manufacturing Company, from 1865 to 1903. The building was on the comer of 10th St. & Chestnut. They moved to the Shaw Piano Co. building at 1001-1061 W. 12th St.

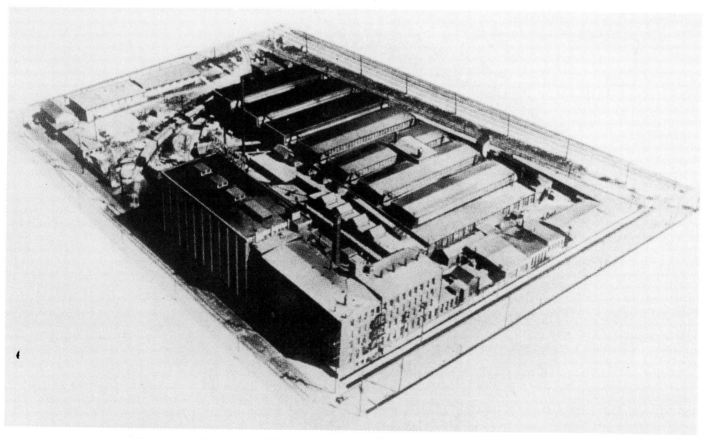

This was the Griswold Manufacturing Company when it closed in 1957.

# TRADE MARKS

## Other Trade Marks that may be found:

1. Colonial Design, "Safety Fill", Cast Aluminum, Erie, PA., U.S.A., Pat'd Sept. 9. 1913. with cross & circle.

2. Griswold, Tite-Top Baster. Printing in a circular pattern.

3. CLASSIC. This was used on a line of stoves.

4. The Griswold Mfg. Co., Cast Iron, Tite-Top Dutch Oven, Erie, PA., U.S.A., Pat' Mar. 16. 20. with cross & circle.

5. **DU•CHRO**

6. KWIK-BAKE. Letters in an outline form.

7. *Aristocraft.* In fancy lettering.

8. Steri-Scald. Both lines of the "S" in Scald extend over & under the other type.

# Griswold Muffin, Corn Bread and Similar Molds

| Number | Pattern No. | No. of Cups | Markings | Variations | |
|---|---|---|---|---|---|
| 1 | ? | 1 | e | 1 | vienna roll, single loaf |
| 1 | 940 | 11 | eG | 2 | round, shallow, square bottom corner |
| 2 | 956 | 2 | e | 1 | vienna roll, double loaf |
| 2 | 941 | 11 | e | 1 | round, shallow, larger than No. 1, round bottom corner |
| 3 | 942 | 11 | eG | 2 | round, shallow |
| 4 | 957 | 4 | e | 1 | vienna roll |
| 5 | 943 | 8 | eG | 2 | oval, shallow |
| 6 | 944 | 12 | eG | 2 | rectangular with rounded corners, shallow |
| 6 | 958 | 6 | eG | 3 | vienna roll (same as later No. 26 958) |
| 7 | 945 | 8 | e | 1 | rectangular with rounded corners, shallow |
| 8 | 946 | 8 | eEG | 3 | round, shallow |
| 9 | 947 | 12* | eG | 4 | round, hemispherical (*early pans had 10 cups) |
| 10 | 948 | 11 | eEG | 5 | round, deep |
| 10 | 949 | 11 | EG | 3 | round, deep |
| 10 | 1253 | 11 | S.R. | 1 | popover pan S.R. & Co., best made for Sears Roebuck & Co. |
| 10 | 1512 | 11 | P,M | 1 | popover pan, Puritan (also Merit) made for Sears Roebuck & Co. |
| 10 | 2010 | 11 | G | 1 | round, deep (top surface is hammered) |
| 11 | ? | 12 | e | 1 | french roll (arrangement of cups is like No. 6 944) |
| 11 | 950 | 12 | eG | 4 | french roll |
| 12 | 951 | 11 | eG | 3 | round, shallow |
| 13 | 640 | 6 | G | 1 | turk head |
| 14 | 641 | 12 | G | 1 | turk head |
| 14 | 952 | 12 | e | 2 | rectangular, shallow |
| 15 | 6138 | 12 | G | 2 | french roll, large |
| 16 | 6139 | 6 | G | 2 | french roll, large |
| 17 | 6140 | 6 | G | 3 | french roll |
| 18 | 6141 | 6 | G | 3 | round, deep. Early pans marked Griswold's Erie |
| 19 | 966 | 6 | eG | 3 | round, hemispherical |
| 20 | 953 | 11 | eG | 2 | turk head, swirled |
| 21 | 961 | 7 | G | 1 | bread stick |
| 22 | 954 | 11 | eG | 3 | bread stick |
| 23 | 955 | 22 | G | 1 | bread stick, divided down center |
| 24 | 957 | 7 | - | 1 | bread stick, identical to No. 21 but not marked Griswold |
| 24 | 959 | 6 | e | 1 | bread pan, cakes |
| 26 | 958 | 6 | G | 1 | vienna roll (same as No. 6 958) |
| 26 | 960 | 2 | e | 1 | bread pan, loaves |
| 27 | 638 | 6 | G | 2 | head of wheat |
| 28 | ? | 1 | e | 1 | bread pan, loaf |
| 28 | 639 | 6 | G | 2 | head of wheat, large |
| 31 | 963 | 7 | eG | 2 | round, hemispherical; Danish Cake Pan, no top rim |
| 32 | 962 | 7 | eG | 4 | round, hemispherical; Apple Cake Pan, has top rim |
| 33 | 2992 | 7 | g | 1 | round, hemispherical; Munk Pan, top rim, no side skirt |
| (34) | 969 | 7 | G | 1 | round, shallow; Plett Pan; slightly different than No. 34 2980 |
| 34 | 2980 | 7 | G | 3 | round, shallow; Plett Pan |
| 50 | 959 | 7 | G | 1 | 6 hearts surrounding 6-pointed star |
| 100 | 960 | 6 | G | 1 | 5 hearts surrounding 5-pointed star |
| 130 | 634 | 6 | G | 1 | turk head |
| 140 | 635 | 12 | G | 1 | turk head |
| 240 | 631 | 12 | G | 1 | turk head; rim around top, cups bigger than No. 130 or 140 |
| 262 | 625 | 7 | G | 1 | corn cob, small |
| 270 | 636 | 7 | G | 1 | corn/wheat combination cob; ears alternate directions |
| 272 | 629 | 7 | G | 2 | corn/wheat combination cob; ears point same direction |
| 273 | 930 | 7 | G | 1 | corn cob |
| 273 | 2073 | 7 | G | 1 | corn cob (top surface is hammered) |
| 280 | 637 | 7 | G | 1 | corn/wheat combination cob, large; alternating ears |
| 282 | 630 | 7 | G | 2 | corn/wheat combination cob, large; ears same way |
| 283 | 931 | 7 | G | 1 | corn cob, large |
| 1270 | 1270 | 7 | S.R. | 1 | head of wheat, same pan is No. 2700 |
| 1270 | 1513 | 7 | P,M | 1 | head of wheat pan, and heads of wheat different than p/n 1270 |
| 2700 | 632 | 7 | G | 1 | head of wheat |
| 2800 | 633 | 7 | G | 1 | head of wheat, large |

61 pans                    105 variations (approximate)

Probably more iron cookware collectors have begun their collecting with a set of Griswold skillets than any other piece or make of iron. That was the beginning of my collection; a matching set of skillets and a dutch oven to cook in. At the start I had no idea where it would lead me.

Almost immediately I became aware that putting together a matched set would involve collecting several different sets, i.e. sets of the different size trademarks and their variations. As a beginner I had no way to know which set I would eventually be able to complete. This table will give the beginner and advanced collector alike an idea of what sizes were made in each variation.

Checks in the table indicate that the skillet was made in that variation. I have verified these skillets by actually seeing them but would like to know of any possible mistakes I might have made. ERIE skillets were definitely made in sizes 5-12 but I cannot be certain that all sizes were made in both the early and late styles, the late style having the rounded bottom edge. The easiest set to complete and the one many collectors try for first is the large TM with smooth bottom. (Courtesy of Steve Stephens.)

| | 0 | 1 | 2 | 3 | 4 | 5 | 6 | 7 | 8 | 9 | 10 | 11 | 12 | 13 | 14 | 20 |
|---|---|---|---|---|---|---|---|---|---|---|---|---|---|---|---|---|
| ERIE/spider | | | | | | | | | ✓ | | | | | | | |
| ERIE | | | | | | ✓ | ✓ | ✓ | ✓ | ✓ | ✓ | ✓ | | | | |
| GRISWOLD'S ERIE | | | | | | ✓ | ✓ | ✓ | ✓ | ✓ | ✓ | ✓ | | | | |
| slant TM/ERIE | | ✓ | ✓ | ✓ | ✓ | ✓ | ✓ | ✓ | ✓ | ✓ | ✓ | ✓ | ✓ | ✓ | | |
| slant TM/ERIE PA USA (w/heat ring) | | | ✓ | ✓ | ✓ | ✓ | ✓ | ✓ | ✓ | ✓ | ✓ | ✓ | ✓ | ✓ | | |
| slant TM/ERIE PA USA (smooth bottom) | | | ✓ | | ✓ | | | ✓ | | | | | | | | |
| block TM w/heat ring | ✓ | | ✓ | ✓ | ✓ | ✓ | ✓ | ✓ | ✓ | ✓ | ✓ | ✓ | ✓ | ✓ | ✓ | ✓ |
| block TM smooth bottom | | | ✓ | ✓ | ✓ | ✓ | ✓ | ✓ | ✓ | ✓ | | | | | | |
| sm TM w/early handle | | | | ✓ | | ✓ | ✓ | ✓ | ✓ | ✓ | ✓ | | ✓ w/heat ring | | | |
| sm TM w/late handle | | | | ✓ | ✓ | ✓ | ✓ | ✓ | ✓ | ✓ | ✓ | | | | | |
| sm TM w/late grooved handle | | | | ✓ | ✓ | ✓ | ✓ | ✓ | ✓ | ✓ | ✓ | | | | | |
| late, large TM | | | | ✓ | | | | | | | | | | | | |
| wood handle | | | | ✓ | ✓ | ✓ | ✓ | ✓ | ✓ | ✓ | ✓ | ✓ | ✓ | ✓ | | |
| VICTOR | | | | | | ✓ | ✓ | ✓ | ✓ | ✓ | | | | | | |
| sm TM w/hinge for cover | | | | ✓ | | ✓ | ✓ | ✓ | ✓ | ✓ | | | | | | |

NOTES:

1. ERIE 'early' verified in sizes 6, 7, 8, 9, 10, 11; ERIE 'late' verified in sizes 7, 8, 11.

2. All skillets I have seen larger than size 10 have had a heat ring.

3. Griswold catalog No. 55, Bulletin E-10 (Aug. 1926) shows that wood handle skillets in sizes 2-12 were made.

4. The "late, large TM" in table was used on quite a few pieces at the end of production in Erie, PA. It is the trademark that appears on the Erie-made square skillet with the handle on the side. Many pieces using this TM were porcelainized.

5. The skillets shown in the above table are all black iron and were produced in Erie, PA. Many of these skillets were available in nickel, chrome, or porcelainized finishes.

6. VICTOR skillets were made as early as the ERIE skillets but probably only in sizes 7-9. Size 6 was added sometime in the 1920's and size 5 around 1930.

7. No. 1 skillet is virtually the same size as No. 0 skillet and is possibly an earlier version of the No. 0 skillet which was sold as a toy.

# PRICE GUIDE TO SKILLET CHART

| | | |
|---|---|---|
| ERIE/spider | No. 8 | $ 500-1000 |

| | | |
|---|---|---|
| ERIE | No. 5 | $ 100-200 |
| ERIE | No. 6 | $ 40-75 |
| ERIE | No. 7 | $ 20-40 |
| ERIE | No. 8 | $ 20-40 |
| ERIE | No. 9 | $ 20-40 |
| ERIE | No. 10 | $ 50-75 |
| ERIE | No. 11 | $ 100-200 |
| ERIE | No. 12 | $ 75-150 |

| | | |
|---|---|---|
| GRISWOLD'S ERIE | No. 5 | $ 100-200 |
| GRISWOLD'S ERIE | No. 6 | $ 40-75 |
| GRISWOLD'S ERIE | No. 7 | $ 30-50 |
| GRISWOLD'S ERIE | No. 8 | $ 30-50 |
| GRISWOLD'S ERIE | No. 9 | $ 30-50 |
| GRISWOLD'S ERIE | No. 10 | $ 50-75 |
| GRISWOLD'S ERIE | No. 11 | $ 100-200 |
| GRISWOLD'S ERIE | No. 12 | $ 75-150 |

| | | |
|---|---|---|
| Slant/ERIE | No. 1 | $1000-1500 |
| Slant/ERIE | No. 2 | $ 175-250 |
| Slant/ERIE | No. 3 | $ 20-35 |
| Slant/ERIE | No. 4 | $ 45-75 |
| Slant/ERIE | No. 5 | $ 35-50 |
| Slant/ERIE | No. 6 | $ 30-45 |
| Slant/ERIE | No. 7 | $ 25-40 |
| Slant/ERIE | No. 8 | $ 20-35 |
| Slant/ERIE | No. 9 | $ 25-40 |
| Slant/ERIE | No. 10 | $ 40-70 |
| Slant/ERIE | No. 11 | $ 100-150 |
| Slant/ERIE | No. 12 | $ 60-100 |
| Slant/ERIE | No. 13 | $ 400-500 |
| Slant/ERIE | No. 14 | $ 400-500 |

| | | |
|---|---|---|
| Slant/ERIE PA USA (w/heat ring) | No. 2 | $ 225-250 |
| Slant/ERIE PA USA (w/heat ring) | No. 3 | $ 20-35 |
| Slant/ERIE PA USA (w/heat ring) | No. 4 | $ 50-80 |
| Slant/ERIE PA USA (w/heat ring) | No. 5 | $ 30-55 |
| Slant/ERIE PA USA (w/heat ring) | No. 6 | $ 35-50 |
| Slant/ERIE PA USA (w/heat ring) | No. 7 | $ 30-45 |
| Slant/ERIE PA USA (w/heat ring) | No. 8 | $ 25-40 |
| Slant/ERIE PA USA (w/heat ring) | No. 9 | $ 30-45 |
| Slant/ERIE PA USA (w/heat ring) | No. 10 | $ 45-75 |
| Slant/ERIE PA USA (w/heat ring) | No. 11 | $ 125-175 |
| Slant/ERIE PA USA (w/heat ring) | No. 12 | $ 70-115 |
| Slant/ERIE PA USA (w/heat ring) | No. 13 | $ 450-550 |
| Slant/ERIE PA USA (w/heat ring) | No. 14 | $ 450-650 |

| | | |
|---|---|---|
| Slant/ERIE PA USA (w/smooth bottom) | No. 2 | $ 250-300 |
| Slant/ERIE PA USA (w/smooth bottom) | No. 5 | $ 25-40 |
| Slant/ERIE PA USA (w/smooth bottom) | No. 8 | $ 20-35 |

| | | |
|---|---|---|
| Block TM w/heat ring | No. 0 | $ 50-90 |
| Block TM w/heat ring | No. 2 | $ 300-400 |
| Block TM w/heat ring | No. 3 | $ 25-35 |
| Block TM w/heat ring | No. 4 | $ 100-200 |
| Block TM w/heat ring | No. 5 | $ 75-120 |
| Block TM w/heat ring | No. 6 | $ 30-45 |
| Block TM w/heat ring | No. 7 | $ 25-40 |
| Block TM w/heat ring | No. 8 | $ 20-35 |
| Block TM w/heat ring | No. 9 | $ 25-40 |
| Block TM w/heat ring | No. 10 | $ 40-60 |
| Block TM w/heat ring | No. 11 | $ 125-175 |
| Block TM w/heat ring | No. 12 | $ 75-115 |
| Block TM w/heat ring | No. 13 | $ 500-600 |
| Block TM w/heat ring | No. 14 | $ 75-150 |
| Block TM w/heat ring | No. 20 | $ 350-450 |

| | | |
|---|---|---|
| Block TM w/smooth bottom | No. 2 | $ 200-300 |
| Block TM w/smooth bottom | No. 3 | $ 10-20 |
| Block TM w/smooth bottom | No. 4 | $ 30-50 |
| Block TM w/smooth bottom | No. 5 | $ 15-20 |
| Block TM w/smooth bottom | No. 6 | $ 15-20 |
| Block TM w/smooth bottom | No. 7 | $ 15-20 |
| Block TM w/smooth bottom | No. 8 | $ 10-20 |
| Block TM w/smooth bottom | No. 9 | $ 15-25 |
| Block TM w/smooth bottom | No. 10 | $ 40-70 |

| | | |
|---|---|---|
| Small TM w/early handle | No. 3 | $ 5-12 |
| Small TM w/early handle | No. 5 | $ 10-15 |
| Small TM w/early handle | No. 6 | $ 10-15 |
| Small TM w/early handle | No. 7 | $ 10-15 |
| Small TM w/early handle | No. 8 | $ 10-15 |
| Small TM w/early handle | No. 9 | $ 15-20 |
| Small TM w/early handle | No. 10 | $ 20-35 |
| Small TM w/early handle (w/heat ring) | No. 12 | $ 50-85 |

| | | |
|---|---|---|
| Small TM w/late handle | No. 3 | $ 5-12 |
| Small TM w/late handle | No. 4 | $ 20-35 |
| Small TM w/late handle | No. 5 | $ 10-15 |
| Small TM w/late handle | No. 6 | $ 10-15 |
| Small TM w/late handle | No. 7 | $ 10-15 |
| Small TM w/late handle | No. 8 | $ 10-15 |
| Small TM w/late handle | No. 9 | $ 15-20 |
| Small TM w/late handle | No. 10 | $ 20-35 |

| | | |
|---|---|---|
| Small TM w/grooved handle | No. 3 | $ 5-12 |
| Small TM w/grooved handle | No. 4 | $ 20-35 |
| Small TM w/grooved handle | No. 5 | $ 10-15 |
| Small TM w/grooved handle | No. 6 | $ 10-15 |
| Small TM w/grooved handle | No. 7 | $ 10-15 |
| Small TM w/grooved handle | No. 8 | $ 10-15 |
| Small TM w/grooved handle | No. 9 | $ 15-20 |
| Small TM w/grooved handle | No. 10 | $ 20-35 |

| | | |
|---|---|---|
| Late, large TM | No. 3 | $ 10-20 |

| | | |
|---|---|---|
| Wood handle | No. 2 | $ 400-500 |
| Wood handle | No. 3 | $ 125-200 |
| Wood handle | No. 4 | $ 125-200 |
| Wood handle | No. 5 | $ 75-125 |
| Wood handle | No. 6 | $ 75-125 |
| Wood handle | No. 7 | $ 40-75 |
| Wood handle | No. 8 | $ 40-75 |
| Wood handle | No. 9 | $ 50-85 |
| Wood handle | No. 10 | $ 75-100 |
| Wood handle | No. 11 | $ 125-200 |
| Wood handle | No. 12 | $ 125-200 |

| | | |
|---|---|---|
| VICTOR | No. 5 | $ 150-200 |
| VICTOR | No. 6 | $ 60-110 |
| VICTOR | No. 7 | $ 35-50 |
| VICTOR | No. 8 | $ 35-50 |
| VICTOR | No. 9 | $ 35-50 |

| | | |
|---|---|---|
| Small Tm w/hinge for cover | No. 3 | $ 20-35 |
| Small Tm w/hinge for cover | No. 5 | $ 20-40 |
| Small Tm w/hinge for cover | No. 6 | $ 20-40 |
| Small Tm w/hinge for cover | No. 7 | $ 15-35 |
| Small Tm w/hinge for cover | No. 8 | $ 15-35 |
| Small Tm w/hinge for cover | No. 9 | $ 20-40 |

## ROUND BOTTOM KETTLES

Cast iron, extra finish, regular.

| Nos. | 7 | 8 | 9 |
|---|---|---|---|
| Diameter top, inches | 9½ | 10⅝ | 11½ |
| Diameter bottom, inches | 7¾ | 8¾ | 9¾ |
| Depth, inches | 7¼ | 8 | 8½ |
| Capacity, quarts | 6 | 8 | 10½ |
| Each | $2.86 | 3.26 | 4.04 |

## SKILLETS

Cast iron, extra finish, iron handle, extra deep.

| Nos. | 8 | 9 | 10 |
|---|---|---|---|
| Diameter top, inches | 11 | 12 | 12⅜ |
| Diameter bottom, inches | 8¾ | 9½ | 10¼ |
| Depth, inches | 3 | 3 | 3 |
| Each | $1.82 | 2.08 | 2.46 |

## FLAT BOTTOM KETTLES

Cast iron, extra finish.

| Nos. | 7 | 8 | 9 |
|---|---|---|---|
| Diameter top, inches | 9¼ | 10 | 10¾ |
| Diameter bottom, inches | 8¼ | 8⅞ | 9⅝ |
| Depth, inches | 6⅛ | 6½ | 6⅞ |
| Capacity, quarts | 6 | 7 | 9 |
| Each | $2.86 | 3.26 | 4.04 |

## DUTCH OVENS

Trivet

Cast iron, ground joint between body and cover. Self-locking bail; self-basting rings on inside of cover; side handle for pouring. Non-breakable steel trivets, tinned finish.

| Nos. | 7 | 8 | 9 |
|---|---|---|---|
| Diameter top, inches | 9¼ | 10⅛ | 11¼ |
| Diameter bottom, inches | 8 | 9 | 9¾ |
| Depth, inches | 3¾ | 4 | 4¼ |
| Capacity, quarts | 3½ | 4½ | 6 |
| Each | $3.12 | 3.60 | 4.08 |
| Extra covers, each | 1.08 | 1.20 | 1.44 |
| Extra trivets, each | .46 | .56 | .64 |

| Nos. | 10 | 11 | 12 | 13 |
|---|---|---|---|---|
| Diameter top, inches | 12¼ | 13¼ | 14¼ | 15¼ |
| Diameter bottom, inches | 10¾ | 11½ | 12 | 12¾ |
| Depth, inches | 4⅞ | 6 | 7 | 8 |
| Capacity, quarts | 8 | 12 | 15 | 20½ |
| Each | $5.40 | 7.20 | 8.40 | 9.60 |
| Extra covers, each | 1.68 | 2.16 | 2.40 | |
| Extra trivets, each | 1.00 | 1.08 | | |

## GRISWOLD OVENS

Polished steel body; electric welded; corrugated tin lining; asbestos lined; two electric welded wire racks; nickel Alaska handles and door catches; triple glass drop door. Height 16½ inches; width 21 inches; depth 12⅜ inches.

No. 140—Each ........................................................ $6.00

One in a crate

Polished steel body; electric welded; corrugated tin lining; asbestos lined; two electric welded wire racks; nickel Alaska handles and door catches; single glass drop door. Height 16½ inches; width 13¼ inches; depth 12⅜ inches.

No. 125—Each ........................................................ $5.00

One in a crate

## GRISWOLD OVENS

Polished steel body; electric welded swing door; double side walls; two electric welded wire racks. Height 11⅛ inches; width 12⅛ inches; depth 10⅛ inches.

No. 155—Glass door. Each .............................. $2.40

No. 150—Steel door. Each .............................. 2.30

Four in a carton

## GRISWOLD ELEVATED HOT PLATES

Cast iron, black enamel finish; cast-in grates; two single 4-inch star drilled burners; white porcelain handle lever valves; ⅜-inch black enameled manifold; stationary legs; one pan. Size of top 9½x19½ inches; height 20 inches.

No. 2020DLV—Each ........................................ $5.00

## WAFFLE IRONS

"American" Pattern.

Cast iron, extra finish, low frame.

| Nos. | 7 | 8 | 9 |
|---|---|---|---|
| Diameter of pan, inches | 6¾ | 7¾ | 8½ |
| Diameter bottoms of ring, inches | 8¾ | 9⅞ | 10⅝ |
| Each | $1.92 | 2.16 | 2.80 |

## WAFFLE IRONS

Heart-Star.

Cast iron, extra finish, low frame.

| No. | 18 |
|---|---|
| Each | $2.20 |

## WAFFLE IRONS

"American" Pattern.
Cast iron, extra finish, high frame.

| No. | 11 |
|---|---|
| Size of pan, inches | 6¾ x 6¾ |
| Size of cake, inches | 3⅛ x 3⅛ |
| Size of frame, inches | 9¾ x 9¾ |
| Each | $3.10 |

## GRISWOLD MEAT CHOPPERS

Cast iron one-piece frame; spiral feed screw, all cast parts of highest quality iron, doubly coated with pure block tin.

| No. | Size | Capacity Per Min., Lbs. | Dozen |
|---|---|---|---|
| 1 | Small | 2½ | $30.00 |
| 2 | Regular | 3 | 36.00 |
| 3 | Large | 3½ | 41.60 |
| 4 | Hotel | 4 | 54.00 |

## GRISWOLD STUFFER ATTACHMENT

| No. | 1 | 2 | 3 | 4 |
|---|---|---|---|---|
| Dozen | $6.00 | 6.00 | 8.00 | 8.00 |

# 1939 CATALOG PAGE

## ARISTROCRAFT WARE
### GRISWOLD

Made of stain-resisting metal in beautiful streamline design; light weight, yet strong and will last a lifetime; outside is highly polished, with satin silver-smooth inside and natural walnut handles set in bakelite ferrules; smooth flat bottoms are ideal for gas and electric stove cooking; self-basting covers and lips designed for no-drip pouring; each utensil packed in an attractive carton.

### TEA KETTLES

| No. | 1534 | 1535 |
|---|---|---|
| Capacity, quarts | 4 | 5 |
| Wgt. each, lbs. | 4¼ | 4¾ |
| Each | $8.15 | 8.80 |
| Retail Price | $5.50 | 5.95 |

*One in a carton.*

### COVERED SAUCE PANS

| No. | 1512 | 1513 |
|---|---|---|
| Capacity, qts. | 2 | 3 |
| Wgt. each, lbs. | 3⅛ | 4½ |
| Each | $5.80 | 7.35 |
| Retail Price | $3.95 | 4.95 |

*One in a carton.*

### CHICKEN FRYERS

*Retail Price $6.25*

| No. | 128 |
|---|---|
| Inside diameter, in. | 10¼ |
| Wgt. each, lbs. | 4⅝ |
| Each | $9.35 |

*One in a carton.*

### COVERED SKILLET

| No. | 1206 | 1208 |
|---|---|---|
| Inside diam. inches | 8 | 10¼ |
| Wgt. each, lbs. | 3¼ | 4⁹⁄₁₆ |
| Each | $6.60 | 8.15 |
| Retail Price | 4.50 | 5.50 |

*One in a carton.*

★*For shipment from factory a Buffalo, N. Y.*

## ARISTROCRAFT WARE
### GRISWOLD

### OVAL ROASTERS

*Retail Price $9.50*

| No. | 1485 |
|---|---|
| Depth, inches | 4⁷⁄₁₆ |
| Width, in. | 9¾ |
| Length, in. | 12¾ |
| Wgt. each, lbs. | 7½ |
| Each | $13.95 |

*One in a carton.*

### DUTCH OVEN

*Retail Price $6.50*

| No. | 1465 |
|---|---|
| Capacity, qts. | 5 |
| Wgt. each, lbs. | 5¹¹⁄₁₆ |
| Each | $9.55 |

*One in a carton.*

### WOOD HANDLE GRIDDLE

*Retail Price $3.95*

| No. | 1309 |
|---|---|
| Top diam., in. | 10 |
| Wgt. ea., lbs. | 3⁹⁄₁₆ |
| Each | $7.35 |

*One in a carton.*

### PLATTERS WITH TRAYS

| No. | 2082 | 2083 |
|---|---|---|
| Length, in. | 16 | 18 |
| Width, in. | 11¼ | 12½ |
| Wgt. ea., lbs. | 4⁵⁄₁₆ | 5 |
| Each | $5.80 | 7.35 |
| Retail Price | 3.95 | 4.95 |

*One in a carton.*

## CAST ALUMINUM WARE
### GRISWOLD

### TEA KETTLES

Highly polished cast aluminum; colonial pattern; easy-filling spout; ebonized wood bail grip; flat bottom; diameter of bottom, 9¾ in.; capacity 6 quarts.

| No. 8 | Each $8.05 |
|---|---|

*Wgt. each, 5 lbs.; one in a carton.*

# 1939 CATALOG PAGE

## CAST IRON WAFFLE IRONS

**High Base**

For gas and vapor stoves. Cast iron; japanned rim; bright finish molds; spiral wire handles; molds revolve in ball sockets.

| | |
|---|---|
| No. | **28** |
| Diameter molds, inches | 7¾ |
| Diam. bottom ring, inches | 11⅛ |
| Weight each, lbs. | 13 |
| Each | **$3.30** |

*Packed loose.*

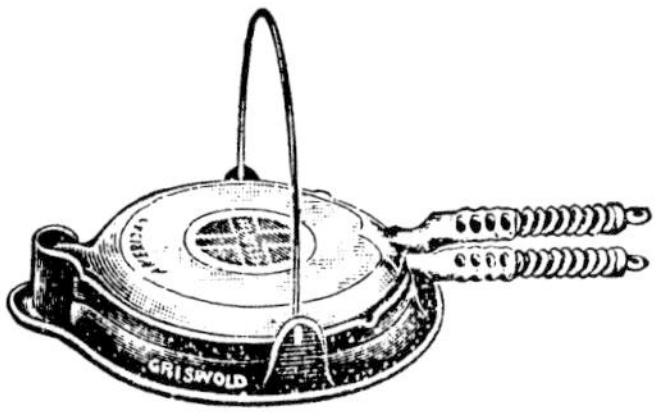


**GRISWOLD**
**Low Base**

Cast iron; japanned rim; bright finish molds; spiral wire handles; molds revolve in ball sockets; diameter of molds, 7¾ in.; diameter of bottom ring, 10 inches.

**No. 18** ................................ Each **$2.42**

*Weight each, 9 lbs.; packed loose.*

## CAST IRON SKILLETS

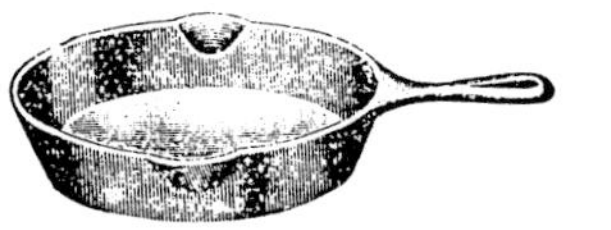

**GRISWOLD**

Genuine Griswold, regular pattern; iron handle; polished inside.

| No. | **103** | **105** | **106** | **107** |
|---|---|---|---|---|
| Top, inches | 6½ | 8 | 9⅛ | 9⅞ |
| Bottom, inches | 5¼ | 6¾ | 7½ | 8¼ |
| Depth,, inches | 1¼ | 1¾ | 1⅞ | 2 |
| Weight each, lbs. | 1⅜ | 2⅜ | 2⅞ | 3¼ |
| Each | **$0.65** | **1.10** | **1.20** | **1.25** |

| No. | **108** | **109** | **110** | **112** |
|---|---|---|---|---|
| Top, inches | 10⅝ | 11⅜ | 11¾ | 13 1/16 |
| Bottom, inches | 8⅞ | 9½ | 10 | 11¾ |
| Depth, inches | 2 | 2 | 2⅛ | 2¼ |
| Weight each, lbs. | 3⅝ | 4⅞ | 5⅛ | 6¾ |
| Each | **$1.05** | **1.65** | **1.85** | **2.50** |

*No. 112 two, all other numbers four in a carton.*

## CAST IRON DUTCH OVENS

**GRISWOLD TITE-TOP**

Self-basting, new style sanitary cover; trivet furnished with each; bail handle; ground joint between body and cover; self-basting rings on inside of cover; self-locking bail; side handle for pouring.

| No. | **DO8** | **DO9** | **DO10** | **DO11** |
|---|---|---|---|---|
| Top, inches | 10⅛ | 11¼ | 12¼ | 13¼ |
| Bottom, inches | 9 | 9¾ | 10¾ | 11½ |
| Depth, inches | 4 | 4¼ | 4⅞ | 6 |
| Quarts | 4½ | 6 | 8 | 12 |
| In crate | 6 | 6 | 5 | 5 |
| Weight each, lbs. | 10½ | 14 | 18 | 23 |
| Each | **$3.55** | **4.75** | **6.10** | **7.55** |

## CHROMIUM CAST IRON WARE

**GRISWOLD**

**SKILLETS ONLY**

Inside of skillet dull finish; top of handle, sides and rim highly polished, full chrome finish; out-side bottom, dull finish.

| No. | **P3** | **P6** | **P7** | **P8** | **P9** |
|---|---|---|---|---|---|
| Top, in. | 6½ | 9⅛ | 9⅞ | 10⅝ | 11⅜ |
| Bottom, in. | 5¼ | 7½ | 8¼ | 8⅞ | 9½ |
| Depth, in. | 1¼ | 1⅞ | 2 | 2 | 2 |
| Wgt. each, lbs. | 1⅜ | 3¼ | 3¾ | 4½ | 5 |
| Each | $1.45 | 2.55 | 2.70 | 2.45 | 3.10 |

*Four in a shipping carton.*

**SKILLET COVERS ONLY**

Outside edge of cover and top of cover handle highly polished full chrome finish; balance not polished; dome shape; self basting.

| No. | **PC6** | **PC7** | **PC8** | **PC9** |
|---|---|---|---|---|
| Diameter, inches | 9⅛ | 9⅞ | 10⅝ | 11⅜ |
| Weight each, lbs. | 2¾ | 4 | 4½ | 5¼ |
| Each | $2.15 | 2.25 | 2.40 | 2.60 |

*Four in a shipping carton.*

**DUTCH OVENS**

Inside of Dutch oven, outside edge of cover and top of handle highly polished chrome finish; outside and bottom of oven and balance of cover not polished; trivet furnished with each; clean easy, self-basting dome shaped cover.

| No. | **PDO8** | **PDO9** |
|---|---|---|
| Top, inches | 10⅛ | 11¼ |
| Bottom, inches | 9 | 9¾ |
| Depth, inches | 4 | 4¼ |
| Capacity, quarts | 4½ | 6 |
| Weight each, lbs. | 12½ | 13 |
| Each | $7.25 | 7.75 |

*One in a carton.*

## STEEL SPIDERS

**NEVER-BREAK**

Stamped from one piece cold rolled wrought steel; highly polished; double lip; handle has hole for hanging. Pan will not absorb grease, scale or warp.

| No. | **NB8** | **NB9** | **NB10** |
|---|---|---|---|
| Diameter bottom, inches | 8 | 9 | 10 |
| Depth, inches | 2¼ | 2¼ | 2¼ |
| Weight per dozen, lbs. | 36¾ | 48 | 51 |
| Per dozen | $14.10 | 16.50 | 18.35 |

*Packed loose.*

## CAST IRON SKILLETS

### GRISWOLD DOUBLE HINGED

**Silverlike Finish**

Pure cast iron with a beautiful silverlike finish; inside is smooth highly polished; can be used as two separate skillets, a chicken fryer, roaster, dutch oven or a deep fat fryer; is ideal for frying, baking or roasting on top of stove or in oven.

Bottom skillet 10¼ in. diameter; 3 in. deep; top skillet 9 15/16 in. diameter, 2 in. deep.

No. 80 . . . . . . . . . . . . . Each **$3.50**
*Weight each, 9½ lbs.; packed loose.*

### REGULAR PATTERN SKILLETS

#### GRISWOLD SILVERLIKE

Pure cast iron with a beautiful silverlike finish; inside is smooth, highly polished; diameter 10¼ in., depth 3 inches.

No. 808 . . . . . . . . . . . . . Each **$1.30**
*Weight each, 3½ lbs.; four in a carton.*

## CAST IRON SKILLET COVERS

### GRISWOLD, SELF-BASTING

Cast Iron; High Quality; Regular Pattern.

| No. | C7 | C8 | C9 | C10 | C12 |
|---|---|---|---|---|---|
| Diameter, inches.... | 9⅞ | 10⅝ | 11⅜ | 11¾ | 12⅞ |
| Weight each, lbs..... | 3 | 3 | 4 | 4½ | 5¼ |
| Each . . . . . . . . . . . | $0.90 | .95 | 1.20 | 1.30 | 1.85 |

*Four in a shipping carton.*

## CAST IRON CHICKEN FRYERS

### GRISWOLD

Especially adapted for frying chicken.

High grade cast iron; polished inside; iron handle; self-basting cover; diameter of top, 10⅝ in.; diameter of bottom, 8¾ inches; depth 3 inches.

No. 138 . . . . . . . . . . . . . . . . . . . . . . Each **$2.65**
*Weight each, 10½ lbs.; one in a carton.*

## CAST IRON CORN STICKS

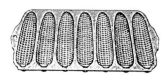

### GRISWOLD

Cast iron, extra finish; for 7 corn sticks.

| No. | 273 | 283 |
|---|---|---|
| Size over all, inches | 13¼ x 5 11/16 | 15 x 6¾ |
| Size of cake, inches | 5⅜ x 1½ | 6 7/16 x 1¾ |
| Weight each, lbs. | 3¾ | 5 |
| Each | $0.90 | 1.10 |

*Four in a carton.*

## CAST IRON GRIDDLES

### GRISWOLD

**Handled**

Best quality cast iron; polished top.

| No. | H108 | H109 |
|---|---|---|
| Diameter, inches | 9⅛ | 10½ |
| Weight each, lbs. | 3¼ | 4¾ |
| Each | $1.30 | 1.45 |

*Packed loose.*

### GOOD HEALTH

**Handled**

High grade cast iron; ground top.

| No. | GH88 |
|---|---|
| Diameter, inches | 9⅛ |
| Weight each, lbs. | 4 |
| Each | $1.10 |

*Four in a carton.*

### GRISWOLD

**Bailed**

High grade, polished top; wire bail; diameter of top, 11½ inches.

No. B112 . . . . . . . . Each **$1.95**
*Weight each, 6 lbs.; packed loose.*

### GRISWOLD

**Long**

High grade, plain (not polished); size 19x8½ inches.

No. 1128 . . . . . . . . . . . . . . . . . . . . . . . . Each **$1.85**
*Weight each, 8 lbs.; packed loose.*

### GRISWOLD

#### Combination Meat and Food Chopper

Cast iron body doubly coated with pure block tin, and funnel shaped; case hardened, four blade rotating knife and block knife plates are reversible and self-sharpening; so constructed that the juices of meats, vegetables, etc., are not squeezed out passing through the web as in the ordinary chopper; easily cleaned.

| No. | 1G | 2G | 3G | 4G |
|---|---|---|---|---|
| Hgt. from table, in. | 5¼ | 6 | 6½ | 7¼ |
| Barrel length, in... | 3 13/32 | 3 19/32 | 3 19/32 | 4 15/32 |
| Diam. hopper, in... | 2½x3¼ | 2¾x3¾ | 3⅛x4¼ | 3⅞x4⅞ |
| Capac. per min., lbs. | 2½ | 3 | 3½ | 4 |
| Wgt. each, lbs.... | 3¾ | 4⅞ | 5¼ | 7½ |
| Per dozen . . . . . . | $29.75 | 35.00 | 41.80 | 47.35 |

*One-twelfth dozen in a box.*

# 1961 CATALOG PAGE

## CAST IRON SKILLET DEALS

### GRISWOLD

Iron ware of the highest quality. Each piece carefully moulded insuring heavier metal where durability and heat are required. Highly polished inside surface, top edge and handle. Treated to prevent rust.

Deal includes 12 skillets and display stand as follows:

| | |
|---|---|
| 2-H50-3G Skillets | 2-H50-7G Skillets |
| 2-H50-5G Skillets | 2-H50-8G Skillets |
| 2-H50-6G Skillets | 2-H50-9G Skillets |

1-Bright Finish Display Stand with Rubber Feet

H50-1760G . . . . . . . . . . . . . . . . . . . . . . . . . . . . . . . . . . . . . . . . . Deal **$61 50**

One deal in shp ctn; wt deal 44 lbs.

---

## CAST HOLLOW WARE

### GRISWOLD ROUND GRIDDLE

Pre-seasoned; ready to use. Diameter 8 inches.

H50-127G . . . . . . . . . . . . . . . . . . . . . . . . . Each **$2 55**
6 in shp ctn; wt each 2 lbs.

### CHICKEN FRYER
**With Self-Basting Covers.**
Close fitting cover with two lips.

| | |
|---|---|
| Diam top, ins . . . . | 10 1/4 |
| Depth, ins . . . . . . | 3 |
| Wt each, lbs . . . . . | 8 1/4 |

H50-328G . . . . . . . . . . . . . . . . . . . . . . . . Each **$12 45**
One in shp ctn; wt each 9 lbs.                    *$5 95*

### GRISWOLD CORN STICK PANS
**Plain Finish**

Bakes delicious corn sticks or cornbread.

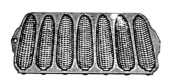

**Size 13 1/4 x 5 3/4 inches**
H50-273 . . . . . . . . . . . . . . . . . . . . . . . . . . Each **$3 75**
One in display box; 4 in shp ctn; wt each 4 lbs.    *$1 75*

---

## CAST HOLLOW WARE

### GRISWOLD, EXTRA FINISH

### GRIDDLES
Cooking surface edge and handle, beautiful high polished finish.
Diameter 10 1/2 inches.

H50-129G . . . . . . . . . . . . . . . . . . . . . Each **$5 70**
4 in shp ctn; wt each 5 lbs.                 *$2 69*

### LONG GRIDDLES
Smooth natural finish.

Length 17 inches; width 9 3/8 inches.

H50-138G . . . . . . . . . . . . . . . . . . . . . . . Each **$10 50**
One in shp ctn; wt each 10 lbs.                 *$ 5 25*

### GRISWOLD – DOUBLE SKILLET

Pre-seasoned extra-finished cast iron. Double hinged.

Bottom skillet – diameter top 10 1/4 inches; depth 3 inches.

Top skillet diameter top 9 15/16 inches; depth 2 inches.

H50-80G . . . . . . . . . . . . . . . . . . . . . . . Each **$14 55**
One in shp ctn; wt each 12 lbs.                 *$6 95*

## GLASS COVERS
**Fits All Griswold Skillets and Other Utensils**
Heatproof, ovenproof and self-basting. Large flange – seats well on utensil – prevents flavor from escaping.

H50-315C– 8 in. . . . . . . . . . . . . . . . . . . . . . . Each **$1 95**
6 in shp ctn; wt each 1 lbs.     *$0 95*

H50-316C– 9 in. . . . . . . . . . . . . . . . . . . . . . . Each **$2 25**
6 in shp ctn; wt each 2 lbs.     *1 10*

H50-318C – 10 1/2 in. . . . . . . . . . . . . . . . . . Each **$2 85**
6 in shp ctn; wt each 3 lbs.     *1 35*

H50-320C – 11 3/4 in. . . . . . . . . . . . . . . . . . Each **$3 90**
3 in shp ctn; wt each 3 1/2 lbs.     *1 85*

## CAST HOLLOW WARE

### GRISWOLD
### Square Bacon and Egg Skillet
A square type skillet with divisions that separate the bacon from the eggs.
Ideal for frying ham, steaks, hamburgers, or cooking square pan cakes, potato cakes, fritters, etc.
**Size overall 9 x 9 x 1 inches.**

H50-666G . . . . . . . . . . . . . . . . . . . . . . . . . . Each **$4 20**
4 in shp ctn; wt each 3 1/4 lbs.     *1 98*

## LAMB CAKE PAN
**Griswold.**
Pre-seasoned cast iron cooking ware, simply was thoroughly, rinse, dry and utensil is ready to use.
For baking attractive design cakes.
Size: 8 x 5 3/4 inches.

H50-866 . . . . . . . . . . . . . . . . . . . . . . . . . . . Each **$8 25**
One in shp ctn; wt each 7 lbs.

### GRISWOLD

### Skillet Ash Tray
Cast iron with jet black finish; moulded in shape of skillet. Ash tray has a convenient matchholder and two cigarette lips.

Diam tray 4 in.; depth 3/4 in.; over -all length 6 3/4 in.
**H26-00JB** . . . . . . . . . . . . . . . . . . . . . . . Each **$1 26**
One in shp ctn; wt each 7 lbs.     *$0 59*

## CAST HOLLOW WARE
### DUTCH OVEN
### Griswold

High polish finish inside.
Heavy wire bail.
Diameter 10 5/8 inches.

**Pyrex Cover**
H50-318G . . . . . . . . . . . . . . . . . . . . . Each **$12 00**
One in shp ctn; wt each 10 lbs.     *$ 5 75*

**Cast Cover**
H50-308 . . . . . . . . . . . . . . . . . . . . . . . Each **$18 75**
One in shp ctn; wt each 12 lbs.     *$ 8 95*

## SKILLET GRIDDLE
Pre-seasoned, needs no breaking in.
Satin smooth finish, hi-polished handles and top edges.
Easy to use, easy to clean.

H50-109G . . . . . . . . . . . . . . . . . . . . . . Each **$18 75**
4 in shp ctn; wt each 4 1/2 lbs.     *$2 69*

### CAKE GRIDDLES
**Plain Finish**

| | H50-88CG | H50-99CG |
|---|---|---|
| Diam, ins . . . . . . . . . . . . . . . . . | 9 3/4 | 10 3/4 |
| Wt each, lbs . . . . . . . . . . . . . . . | 2 1/4 | 3 1/4 |
| Each . . . . . . . . . . . . . . . . . . . . | $3 00 | 3 30 |

6 in shp bdle.

### GRISWOLD – PATTY MOLDS
Extra finished cast iron ware. Made in shallow and deep patterns in four designs of desirable sizes. Two wire handles with each set of two molds. Furnished in display boxes.

### SHALLOW PATTERN

### Round And Fluted Patterns
Set of two molds; 1 round, diam, 2 5/16 in.; depth 9/16 in.; 1 fluted, diam 3 in.; depth 9/16 in.

H50-401G . . . . . . . . . . . . . . . . . . . . . . Each **$3 90**
One set in display box; 4 sets in shp ctn;     *$1 85*
wt set 2 lbs.

# 1963 CATALOG PAGE

**WYETH Company**
St. Joseph, Mo.

## GRISWOLD CAST STOVE HOLLOW WARE
### EXTRA FINISHED, HIGHLY POLISHED INSIDE, PLAIN SMOOTH FINISH OUTSIDE

### SKILLETS

| Nos. | I—D3E | I—D5E |
|---|---|---|
| SIZE NO. | 3 | 5 |
| DIA. TOP, IN. | 6 1/2 | 8 |
| DIA. BOT., IN. | 5 1/4 | 1/4 |
| DEPTH, IN. | 1 1/4 | 1 3/4 |
| WT., LBS. | 2 | 2 1/2 |
| NO. IN CTN. | 6 | 6 |
| WT. CTN. LBS. | 11 | 17 |
| LIST | $1.35 | $2.29 |
| EACH | ON | CBA |
| LOTS OF 6 | TC | CAT |

| Nos. | I—D6E | I—D7E |
|---|---|---|
| SIZE NO. | 6 | 7 |
| DIA. TOP, IN. | 9 1/8 | 9 5/8 |
| DIA. BOT., IN. | 7 1/2 | 8 1/4 |
| DEPTH, IN. | 1 7/8 | 2 |
| WT. LBS. | 3 | 4 |
| NO. IN CTN. | 6 | 6 |
| WT. CTN., LBS. | 21 | 24 |
| LIST | $2.49 | $2.69 |
| EACH | CEE | CRO |
| LOTS OF 6 | CBN | CEH |

| Nos. | I—D8E | I—D9E |
|---|---|---|
| SIZE NO. | 8 | 9 |
| DIA. TOP, IN. | 10 5/8 | 11 3/8 |
| DIA. BOT., IN. | 8 7/8 | |
| DEPTH, IN. | 2 | 2 |
| WT., LBS. | 4 | 4 1/2 |
| NO. IN CTN. | 6 | 4 |
| WT. CTN., LBS. | 26 | 20 1/4 |
| LIST | $2.29 | $3.39 |
| EACH | CBA | HHE |
| LOTS OF 4 | | HNA |
| LOTS OF 6 | CAR | |

| Nos. | I—D10E | I—D12E |
|---|---|---|
| SIZE NO. | 10 | 12 |
| DIA. TOP, IN. | 11 3/4 | 13 7/8 |
| DIA. BOT., IN. | 10 1/4 | 11 3/4 |
| DEPTH, IN. | 2 1/4 | 2 1/4 |
| WT., LBS. | 5 1/2 | 6 |
| NO. IN CTN. | 2 | 2 |
| WT. CTN. LBS. | 11 3/4 | 15 1/4 |
| LIST | $3.75 | $5.75 |
| EACH | HBN | ATA |
| LOTS OF 2 | HHB | AMB |

### CAST IRON COVERS

GRISWOLD SELF-BASTING FOR GRISWOLD CAST IRON SKILLET.

| No. | I—D145 |
|---|---|
| FOR SKILLET NO. | I—D8E |
| NO. IN CTN. | 2 |
| WT. CTN., LBS. | 9 1/2 |
| LIST | $2.39 |
| EACH | CBO |
| LOTS OF 2 | CMA |

### SKILLET ASSORTMENT
#### GRISWOLD

| I—D239 | $30.00 | CTPN EACH |
|---|---|---|

A PRACTICAL ASSORTMENT, 12 CAST IRON SKILLETS — SIX POPULAR SIZES—2 EACH 3, 5, 6, 7, 8 AND 9. HANDY EYE-CATCHING FREE DISPLAY RACK.
ONE IN CARTON, WT. 44 LBS.

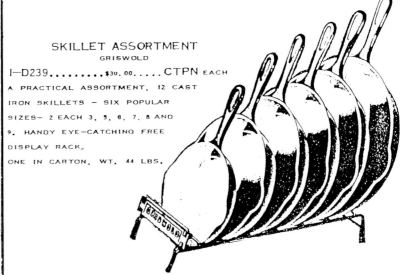

### COVER FOR GRISWOLD CAST SKILLETS

#### GLASS COVER

SELF-BASTING, HEAT RESISTANT GLASS.

| No. | I—D315 | I—D316 |
|---|---|---|
| DIAM., IN. | 8 | 9 |
| FOR SKILLET NO. | 5E | 6E |
| NO. IN CTN. | 6 | 6 |
| WT. CTN., LBS. | 9 | 10 |
| LIST | $0.95 | $1.19 |
| EACH | EA | RO |
| LOTS OF 6 | BR | RC |

| Nos. | I—D318 | I—D320 |
|---|---|---|
| DIAM., IN. | 10 1/2 | 11 3/4 |
| FOR SKILLET NO. | I—D8E | I—D10E |
| FOR DUTCH OVEN NO. | I—D370 | .... |
| NO. IN CTN. | 1 | 3 |
| WT. CTN., LBS. | 2 | 10 |
| LIST | $1.35 | $1.85 |
| EACH | ON | CHA |
| LOTS OF 6 | TC | |
| LOTS OF 3 | ... | CCC |

### HINGED DOUBLE SKILLET

| No. | I—D80 |
|---|---|
| DIAM. BOT., IN. | 10 1/4 |
| DEPTH BOT., IN. | 3 |
| DIA. TOP, IN. | 9 7/8 |
| DEPTH TOP, IN. | 2 |
| WT. CTN., LBS. | 9 1/2 |
| LIST | $6.95 |
| EACH | MCR |

ONE IN CARTON.

# 1963 CATALOG PAGE

**WYETH Company**
St. Joseph, Mo.

## GRISWOLD CAST STOVE HOLLOW WARE
EXTRA FINISHED, HIGHLY POLISHED INSIDE, PLAIN SMOOTH FINISH OUTSIDE

### CHICKEN FRYERS
I—D395.....$5.95.....ABR EACH

DIAM. TOP 10 1/2 IN., DIAM. BOTTOM 9 IN., DEPTH 3 IN. EXTRA FINISHED CAST IRON WITH SELF-BASTING DOME SHAPED COVER.

ONE IN CARTON, WT. 10 1/2 LBS.

### GRISWOLD CHICKEN FRYER
I—D338....$4.99.......ANN EACH

EARLY AMERICAN, 10 1/2 INCH PRE-SEASONED QUALITY CAST IRON. SELF-BASTING, C—THRU COVERS. EXTRA FINISHED COOKING SURFACE WITH POLISHED HANDLE. THE PROPER WEIGHT FOR PERFECT COOKING. EVEN HEATING OVER ENTIRE SURFACE. RETAINS HEAT FOR ECONOMICAL USE. SELF—LUBRICATING SURFACE OF GRISWOLD CAST IRON.

ONE IN CARTON, WT. 6 LBS.

### GRISWOLD CAST DUTCH OVEN WITH COVER
I—D310.....$9.95.....BOR EACH

CHUCK WAGON DUTCH OVEN. COOK FOR THE WHOLE TROOP WHEN CAMPING. 8 QUART CAPACITY. LISTED IN GIRL SCOUT CAMP CATALOG.

ONE IN CARTON, WT. 13 LBS.

#### CAST IRON DUTCH OVENS

WITH SELF-BASTING CAST IRON ENAMELED "CLEAN EASY" COVER, LOCK BAIL AND ALUMINUM TRIVET.

| No. | I—D570 |
|---|---|
| CAP., QTS. | 4 1/2 |
| MEAT CAP., LBS. | 5 TO 7 |
| DIAM. TOP, IN. | 10 1/8 |
| DIAM. BOT., IN. | 9 |
| DEPTH, IN. | 4 |
| WT., LBS. | 12 1/2 |
| LIST, EACH | $8.95 |
| EACH | BAR |

#### CAST IRON DUTCH OVENS

HIGHLY POLISHED INSIDE, WITH PYREX COVER, ALUMINUM TRIVET AND LOCK BAIL.

| No. | I—D370 |
|---|---|
| DIAM. TOP, IN. | 10 1/8 |
| DEPTH, IN. | 4 |
| CAP., QTS. | 4 1/2 |
| MEAT CAP., LBS. | 5 TO 7 |
| WT., LBS. | 8 |
| LIST, EACH | $5.75 |
| EACH | AMB |

ALL NOS. ONE IN CARTON.

### CHEF TYPE SKILLET
GRISWOLD

I—D43.....$1.59...CNE EACH

LOTS OF 6.....OB EACH

9-INCH DIAMETER BOWL SHAPED SIDES MAKE THIS CAST IRON HOLLOW WARE SKILLET THE PERFECT KITCHEN COMPANION.

SIX IN CARTON, WT. 17 LBS.

### SKILLET—GRIDDLE
I—D109.....$2.89.....COA EACH

LOTS OF 4.........CRA EACH

COMBINATION SKILLET AND GRIDDLE, 11 3/8 IN. DIAMETER, WITH SMOOTH FLAT BOTTOM. IDEAL FOR USE ON GAS, ELECTRIC RANGES OR ANY KIND OF FUEL. LIGHT IN WEIGHT, EXCELLENT FOR CHOPS, STEAKS, FISH, GRIDDLE CAKES, ETC.

4 IN CARTON, WT. 13 LBS.

### GRIDDLE
GRISWOLD

I—D127....$1.29....TE EACH

LOTS OF 6......RR EACH

8-INCH DIAMETER MAKES ONE HANDY INDIVIDUAL PANCAKE. PRE-SEASONED CAST IRON. LIFETIME GUARANTEE.

SIX IN CARTON, WT. 14 LBS.

# 1964 CATALOG PAGE

## GRISWOLD'S SYMBOL ALUMINUM COOKWARE

SYMBOL IS CAST AT JUST THE RIGHT THICKNESS FOR PERFECT TEMPERATURE CONTROL IN COOKING. SYMBOL IS BREAK-PROOF...RESISTANT TO DAMAGE FROM KNOCKS AND DROPS, WITHSTANDS ALL COOKING HAZARDS, AND PROMISES MANY YEARS OF UNSURPASSED SERVICE. SYMBOL FEATURES FULL CIRCLE POURING LIP. CATCH RIM THAT PREVENTS BOIL-OVERS. EASY GRIP HANDLES AND COVER KNOBS. STICK RESISTANT INTERIOR FINISH. LEVEL BASE FOR MAXIMUM BURNER CONTACT. PIERCED HANDLES FOR EASY HANGING.

### SKILLETS WITH RED PORCELAIN COVERS

7—D95.— 8-INCH........$8.95..........BOR EACH
ONE IN CARTON, WT. 2 LBS.

7—D96 – 10 INCH.......$8.95.........BOR EACH
ONE IN CARTON, WT. 4 LBS.

### SAUCE PANS WITH RED PORCELAIN COVERS

7—D92 – 2 QT.......$8.95............BOR EACH
ONE IN CARTON, WT. 3 LBS.

7—D93 – 3 QT.......$9.95.............EEA EACH
ONE IN CARTON, WT. 3 LBS.

### TWO—PIECE STARTER SET
### WITH
### INTERCHANGEABLE RED PORCELAIN COVER

7—D350.............$14.95.............OOR EACH

SET CONSISTS OF –

    I — 7D—93 – 3 QT. SAUCEPAN
    I — 7D—95 – 8 IN. SKILLET
    I — INTERCHANGEABLE COVER (RED)

ONE SET IN GIFT BOX. WT. 4 LBS.

### OVAL ROASTER WITH MEAT RACK
### AND
### RED PORCELAIN COVER

7—D99 – 15-INCH.....$14.95........OOR EACH
ONE IN CARTON. WT. 7 LBS.
ROASTER HOLDS 10 LB. FOWL.

### 5 QT. DUTCH OVEN WITH MEAT RACK
### AND
### RED PORCELAIN COVER

7—D98 – 10-INCH.....$11.95.........ROR EACH
ONE IN CARTON. WT. 5 LBS.

## LESS B 0/0 IN LOTS OF 6

# "Dinners cooked on top of the stove in these tight, DRIPPING UTENSILS

### *are rich with nutrition"*

—*says* AUNT ELLEN

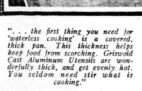

"... the first thing you need for 'waterless cooking' is a covered, thick pan. This thickness helps keep food from scorching. Griswold Cast Aluminum Utensils are wonderfully thick, and get evenly hot. You seldom need stir what is cooking."

"... then the second thing is a cover that fits closely. This holds in the steam—and the flavor. Note that not even the thin blade of a paring knife can get under the Griswold Cover."

"... and of course, for finest cooking, every cover should have drip-rings. These keep the food moist and flavorsome all over. Griswolds are the only covers that are all self-basting like this!* They make a big difference in flavor."

THERE is, for almost any meat, or vegetable, or fruit, one finest way of cooking — that makes it richest in its own flavor, most tender, most nutritious. . . . Cook fruits, vegetables and meats, with very little water, in Griswold thick Cast Aluminum Utensils— and you discover what is believed to be that "finest way" for sixty per cent of the familiar foods.

You conserve all the food's nutrition. These thick utensils require only minimum moisture —and the least flame—you don't dilute the food's fresh savor. There's never enough water for you to drain any of it away. Very little juice is extracted, yet enough to bubble gently—and to drip in steamy richness from the rings inside the cover. This makes a flavorsome liquor around the turkey or roast for gravy . . . around the wax-beans for white sauce. . . . Potatoes seal themselves in a buttery brownness. Beets and peas acquire a brilliance. Apples sit in a fruit syrup. Pork gets so tender it lies back on the carving-knife in thin, flaky slices when you cut it at the table.

Griswold Cast Aluminum Utensils come in beautiful combinations. They stay brightly gleaming; and you can never hurt or dent them. "Waterless" Utensils in both Cast Aluminum and Cast Iron are at hardware, department, house-furnishing stores. Reasonably priced. Write for free copy of "The Aunt Ellen Booklet on Waterless Cooking," with fifty famous recipes by Aunt Ellen. The Griswold Mfg. Co., Dept. A, Erie, Penna.

"... you can cook a White Pork Dinner —the tender pork, the glazed red apple rings, the juicy spinach, the delicate caramel pudding to be served with cream caramel nut sauce—all in this Dutch Oven Steamer, on top of the stove." For the recipe, address "Aunt Ellen," Dept. A, The Griswold Kitchen, Erie, Penna.

"... cook spinach, and beans, and eggs, in the Triplicate Set at one time. It is three utensils for one burner. And toast strips of bread on the triplicate covers, to serve around the chopped eggs and spinach!"

# GRISWOLD

(GRISWOLD)

**Reg. U. S. Pat. Off.**
*Patented and protected.*

© 1927

"... in five minutes this thick coffee-pot makes smooth, fragrant coffee, and will keep it hot for an hour and a half. . . . Or it will keep it frosty-cold that long, if you want chilled coffee to serve with whipped cream that is frozen."

For the most enjoyable fried chicken ever put on a platter . . . that seethes and luxuriates in good things till it gains an exalted flavor!—ask Aunt Ellen for her recipe for Fried Chicken Louisiane. Address "Aunt Ellen," Dept. 1, The Griswold Kitchen, Erie, Pa.

AUNT ELLEN *says :—*

## "When folks praise my fried chicken I smile and think of my Griswold Skillet with its close-fit iron cover."

YOUNG fowl may be tender, but it hasn't much flavor . . . and if it's old enough for flavor, where's the tenderness gone? But here's a way to make old fowl tender as spring chicken, and young fowl tasty as a mother-hen! Fry it in the Griswold Cast Iron Skillet, *under the Griswold close-fit self-basting Cover.* You're frying it, then, in a solid enclosure of moist, dripping heat. All the rich, spattering goodness stays right there. Flavor can't escape. Drippings inside the cover put back on the meat the rich-ness that steams up to the lid and that, uncovered, would be lost. In that slow, close frying, fried chicken, pork chops get delicate and done without danger of scorching. No other skillet, anywhere, fries meats like this! Try one. See Griswold Skillets and Covers at any better class hardware, department or house-furnishing store. The Griswold Mfg. Co., Erie, Pa., U.S.A.

*Makers of Extra-finished Cooking Utensils in Cast Iron and Aluminum, Waffle Irons, Food Choppers, Reversible Stove and Furnace Pipe Dampers, Fruit Presses, Mail Boxes, Bolo and other Portable Bake Ovens and Electric Waffle Bakers.*

# GRISWOLD

★

---

92

*Aunt Ellen Says*

"Look for GRISWOLD TRADEMARK when you buy cast-iron utensils"

Griswold cast iron skillets are sold the country over in the best hardware and department stores.

Corn muffins, pop-overs and all the rest just naturally turn out light and toothsome when cooked in a Griswold cast iron Muffin Pan.

*Dear Mary*

Even if I have cooked with Griswold ware all my life, I always look over the Griswold advertisements in the magazines, and Griswold displays in stores.

When I read that only the purest of iron goes into these utensils, I think—"that's why Griswold things never get battered, wobbly and decrepit." You can use Griswold for years and they just get better and better.

With the cool fall days coming on, you'll be using your Griswold skillet often, for broiling and frying. Snappy weather is "skillet weather." And certainly if I hadn't already sent you one, I'd be sending you a skillet now.

Never hesitate to recommend Griswold ware, Mary. It'll never fail you or your best friend.

Affectionately,

*Aunt Ellen*

## GRISWOLD

 Aunt Ellen's ham steak dinner always makes a hit with her men folk. She'll gladly give you the recipe. Just send in your name on the coupon below.

AUNT ELLEN
DEPT. A, THE GRISWOLD KITCHEN, ERIE, PA.
Please send me your recipe for ham steak dinner.

Name .............................................

Address ...........................................

**1921 Home Journal**

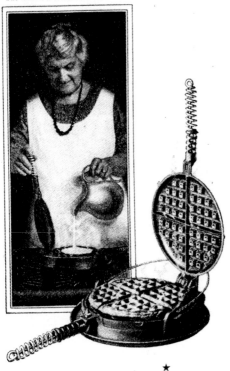

Delicious Confection Waffles . . . golden, tender—with rice in them, chopped-up pecans — and dripping with a velvety hard sauce. . . Ask Aunt Ellen how to make them! Address "Aunt Ellen," Dept. 1, The Griswold Kitchen, Erie, Penna.

Just one of Aunt Ellen's "host of good things" is Aunt Ellen's Hash . . . a glorified deliciousness that comes out like a refined omelet folded in with poached eggs. A more tempting way to serve left-overs than even the initial servings! Ask her about this and address "Aunt Ellen," Dept. O-1, The Griswold Kitchen, Erie, Penna.

## *Aunt Ellen says:*

## "When I give my guests waffles, they invariably come to the kitchen to see my waffle iron.

SOON as they've eaten one waffle, there's another! Crispy gold and tender every time. Of course, my recipe has a lot to do with it, but it's my Griswold Waffle Iron that bakes them so beautifully. The secret is that the Griswold keeps such steady heat *all over*, the waffles get their rich, flaky crusts and melt-away insides quicker'n you can think. The Griswold cooks them fast! And never a waffle sticks." You can get a Griswold Waffle Iron, plain or heart-star design — also Griswold Electric Wafflers—at almost any hardware, department or house-furnishing store. The Griswold Mfg. Co., Erie, Penna., U.S.A.

*Makers of Extra Finished Cooking Utensils in Cast Iron and Aluminum, Waffle Irons, Food Choppers, Reversible Stove and Furnace Pipe Dampers, Fruit Presses, Mail Boxes, Bolo and other Portable Bake Ovens, and Electric Waffle Bakers.*

**March 1926 – Good Housekeeping**

## *Aunt Ellen says:*

## "I make my salads and a host of good things in a jiffy, because my Griswold Combination Meat and Food Chopper cuts, not grinds.

I USED to think that to make an enticing salad, I had to cut up everything by hand. Tedious work! But now I put meats, vegetables, fruits into my Griswold Combination Meat and Food Chopper and watch them come out right, in tiny juicy bits. My Griswold chops these into large, medium, small pieces; and leaves the delicious juices inside each appetizing piece. The Griswold doesn't grind or squeeze. It cuts them as would scissors or a knife. The knives in the Griswold Chopper sharpen themselves and cut cleanly. The revolving plates give the size pieces I like. Fruit acids don't discolor this chopper. And it is everlasting—sturdy as all Griswold Utensils are." See one at any better class hardware, department or house-furnishing store. The Griswold Mfg. Co., Erie, Penna., U.S.A.

*Makers of Extra Finished Cooking Utensils in Cast Iron and Aluminum, Waffle Irons, Food Choppers, Reversible Stove and Furnace Pipe Dampers, Fruit Presses, Mail Boxes, Bolo and other Portable Bake Ovens, and Electric Waffle Bakers.*

**May 1926 – Good Housekeeping**

# GRISWOLD

Reg. U.S.        Pat. Off.

GRISWOLD

# MAGAZINE ADS

*Try baby peas in the Tite-Top Saucepan, cooked in this old honored French way with a whole head of new lettuce, some onions, a mysterious dressing. "Aunt Ellen" will give you her recipe. Address her in care of the Griswold Kitchen, Dept. P, Erie, Penna.*

**N**ow is the time in every garden when nature is urging what to eat. So eat the fresh vegetables — eat them raw or eat them cooked, but cooked with the flavors nature has seasoned them with so gently. . . . What most vegetables need is to be given gentle cooking. Not to have their heads in water. Only to be steamed around quietly. To have a beautiful tolerance paid their flavors, so they can emerge as cooked vegetables, not as simply tender fibres.

Griswold Utensils do just this. They are "Waterless" Utensils — which means they coddle and cherish flavors. Their tight self-basting covers hold the steam in place, and they drip back the flavors that try to steam away.

So eat the green peas "waterless

*Fresh waffles are cooked without grease on the Griswold Electric Heart-Star Baker $10.75. Delightful, crisp hearts and stars. The Baker is also made in regular pattern — same price.*

cooked"—buttered or creamed. Eat the silver onions caramelized around the flank steak. The "Aunt Ellen" Booklet on Waterless Cooking tells many fine ways of cooking. See the Griswold "Waterless" Utensils at kitchen-equipment stores. Beautiful cast aluminum — for the bridal showers on your list. The Griswold Mfg. Co., Dept. P, Erie, Penna. ★

# GRISWOLD

### May 1929 – Good Housekeeping

*Write for Aunt Ellen's "My Meat-Surprising Saucepan Dinner Recipe", also "The Aunt Ellen Booklet on Waterless Cooking", with fifty recipes, a gift that lives her. Address famous The Griswold Kitchen, Erie, Penna.*

**U**se this thick gleaming sauce-pan like any other saucepan, if you like. For peas, applesauce, new potatoes, small roasts. . . . But also "waterless-cook" in it. It is a waterless utensil. You can "waterless-cook" even two or three vegetables at a time, and their flavors will not mingle. When they are served in separate bowls, no one will know they were cooked together, yet you have only the one utensil to wash, and will have used but the one burner.

Also use it as a Tite-Top Dutch Oven, to cook a pot-roast with vegetables. It has drip-rings in the cover, the same as a Griswold Dutch Oven has, and these drip juices, drenching the meat to an unusual tenderness and flavor.

You can do all this with one saucepan, because it is a Griswold Thick Cast Aluminum Saucepan, with a thick cast aluminum cover. Thicker than most utensils are, perfect for heat—and shiny, beautiful, silvery all over. Obtain several sizes at your local hardware, housefurnishing or department store. The Griswold Mfg. Co., Dept. S, Erie, Penna.

# GRISWOLD ★

### October 1929 – Good Housekeeping

# GRISWOLD ★

No matter how remarkable one Griswold Cast Iron Skillet is, one isn't enough. There needs to be a larger, a smaller. . . . Any size Griswold Cast Iron Skillet you buy can have a self-basting cover! Any size can be just the superior cast iron. Or it can be "silverlike"—with a white nickel finish, a clean bright beauty you will like. Or it can be "chinalike" — enameled in jade green, turquoise blue, canary yellow, mandarin red. And the skillets are just thick enough for perfect cooking. Obtain in your local hardware, house-furnishing or department store. Write us for "Aunt Ellen's" cleverest skillet recipe and the "Aunt Ellen Booklet on Waterless Cooking." The Griswold Kitchen, Dept. R, Erie, Pennsylvania.

### September 1929 – Good Housekeeping

**F**or that vastly important world of the kitchen—women who make appearance the basis of selection will delight in having a Griswold "Chinalike" Skillet around—with its self-basting Cover. With this Cover on, the whole utensil looks like lustrous pale blue china. Or like jade green china. Or yellow china—or even a lively red china! It is the Griswold Cast Iron Skillet and Cover that is known so well—enameled. So smooth that it is a pleasure just to touch it.

And when the kitchen world takes on the goodly smells and activities of dinner—women whose greater interest is in how this skillet cooks, and if its cover really bastes—find that they do, perfectly! This is because the enameling that is all over the sides and bottom of the skillet, and over the top of the cover—doesn't alter in any way the perfect cooking for which Griswold Cast Iron Skillets have long been famous.

The "Chinalike" finish stays smooth as glass. It won't chip or crack with ordinary care. It is eminently practical as well as so beautiful—and washes as easily as any china.

Ask to see Griswold "Chinalike" Cast Iron Skillets and Covers in turquoise blue, jade green, canary yellow, and mandarin red. At practically any kitchen-equipment place. Prices are $1.50 to $4.75, including the Cover.

*Do you know Aunt Ellen's newest, finely fragrant, tempting way to cook a round of ham? You should! Ruddy, juicy, new scented, and wholly tender. A free recipe. Also ask for "Aunt Ellen's Booklet on Waterless Cooking" with its famous fifty recipes by Aunt Ellen. Address the Griswold Kitchen, Dept. M, Erie, Penna.*

# ★ GRISWOLD

### February 1929 – Good Housekeeping

216

# This food chopper chops clean

*One of the finest summer cakes we know of is Aunt Ellen's Food Chopper Cake. No baking, just a cooling, and made simply with graham crackers, dates, nuts, and cream. A delectable roll that you slice for serving. Address "Aunt Ellen," Dept. Q, The Griswold Kitchen, Erie, Penna.*

SUMMER servings make clear call for a clean-chopping chopper. Fruit pudding, salad, meat loaf, date-nut cookies, relish, croquettes, Red Flannel Hash. . . . The Griswold Food Chopper chops clean! And it *can* chop a small amount at a time, it will not drip. This is because the handle-end is higher than the chopper-end, and its bowl is deep.

Because it *chops* (there's a difference between that and grinding) each piece still has almost all its juices in it. What little juice is lost by virtue of the incision, is saved in the dish you place in front. Clean chopping —sharp chopping—in medium, large or small pieces. And the Chopper sharpens its own knives.

The Griswold Chopper is a meat chopper, and a nut, fruit, vegetable and bread chopper. It can redeem many a leftover in your refrigerator. It screws into place without marring the table, and is simple and sturdy, as the Griswold restaurant choppers are. At any kitchen-equipment store. In four sizes. $1.85 to $3.25. Write for the Aunt Ellen Booklet of fifty famous recipes—among them French Melange. The Griswold Mfg. Co., Dept. Q, Erie, Penna.

Reg. U. S. Pat. Off. **GRISWOLD ★**

**June 1929 – Good Housekeeping**

---

Trade GRISWOLD Mark

*Write for Aunt Ellen's Thanksgiving menu with recipes for serving a family of six. Also "The Aunt Ellen Booklet on Waterless Cooking" with fifty more recipes. Address the Griswold Kitchen, Erie, Penna.*

HERE is the famous Griswold Tite-Top Dutch Oven. Usually it is in cast iron. Here it is in shining thick cast aluminum—as silvery to look upon as silver itself. It does the same wonderful things as the iron Tite-Top Dutch Oven.

Lift the cover while meat cooks in it, and see the self-basting. There's a constant drip-drip from the rings inside the cover. A rich, important dripping—making the brown skin of roast chicken, the outer slices of roast, drenched and drenched with flavor.

You can't rattle the cover around, for even the thin blade of a knife can't find room to get under. Squab, pork roast with dumplings, stuffed shoulder of lamb—these cook in a tightness of steam that can't escape —that forces them to get tender.

A self-baster, a "waterless cooker," a deep-fat utensil for croquettes, doughnuts—how can kitchens do their best without a Griswold Tite-Top Dutch Oven? Or, at Thanksgiving time, without the Oval Roaster (shown above)? This is a Tite-Top Dutch Oven shaped to fit a turkey. Many sizes, at hardware, department, and house-furnishing stores. The Griswold Mfg. Co., Dept. T, Erie, Penna.

# GRISWOLD ★

**1929 Good Housekeeping**

---

202

Reg. U. S. GRISWOLD Pat. Off.

# If you cook a hot dinner every night

*Write for "Aunt Ellen's" Meat in Leaves recipe. Try as is also her booklet on Waterless Cooking, with fifty more recipes. Address "Aunt Ellen" Dept. O, The Griswold Kitchen, Erie, Penna.*

Do you often tire of the familiar meat servings . . . often wish for some new kind of roast, or steak, or ham? Here's one to all effects; and it will surprise you by its inexpense. It is delicate like quail. And its outer shell is young leaves that stay whitish green as they shine through red tomato sauce.

Little juicy steak-cakes are bundled in cabbage leaves—then steamed in the Griswold Tite-Top Dutch Oven. This is a "Waterless" Dutch Oven. The vegetables and meats you usually boil can now be steamed in it, and their flavors cherished. Steamed safely, gently—with a perpetual self-basting that adds to their tenderness and good rich taste.

*Waffles give a "party" accent to dinners—with the salad, the chicken, or the ice cream. This Griswold Electric Waffle Baker is simple to bake with—and simple to keep clean. $18.75. It is also made in Heart-Star pattern.*

Kitchen-furnishing stores have Griswold "Waterless" Utensils. Cast aluminum, beautiful to cook with, to wash, to keep hanging in sight in your kitchen. The Griswold Mfg. Co., Dept. O, Erie, Penna.

★ **GRISWOLD**

**April 1929 – Good Housekeeping**

---

203

# A dinner for a hungry child

THE clear shining light in a child's eyes when he views this dinner will keep on being clear and shining after he has eaten these fresh vegetables—for they are that kind of vegetables.

Carrots — cooked this new fine way. Potatoes — with a new and exclaimed-about flavor. Spinach that puts iron into those slender limbs — not ordinary spinach by any means. Then with a poached egg, a glass of milk, a cookie or apple—it is one good dinner!

The vegetables are cooked as you perhaps have never cooked them—seasoned perhaps as you have never seasoned them . . . in this, the Griswold Triplicate Set. It is a "waterless" set, and it coddles the vegetables in gentle steam. It holds in all the nutrition that vegetables are famed for, while cherishing and concentrating their flavors. Even what tries to escape as steam gets basted back from the rings in the cover. Then with "Aunt Ellen's" special way of seasoning—well, the need of most vegetables is for just such cooking, just as the need of most children is for just such vegetables.

Griswold "Waterless" Utensils are in glinting thick cast aluminum, in many shapes and sizes. See them at any kitchen-equipment store.

*Write for "Aunt Ellen's" recipe for a vegetable dinner for children. Also for her booklet on "Waterless Cooking"—with its fifty recipes more. Address "Aunt Ellen," Dept. N, The Griswold Kitchen, Erie, Penna.*

★ **GRISWOLD** Reg. U. S. Pat. Off.

**March 1929 – Good Housekeeping**

## The Griswold HEART-STAR

*Waffle Iron*

"*HAVE a heart!*" urges Mother, generously, never intending to be slangy, bless her!

But what else can she say when she is making waffles on a Griswold Heart-Star Waffle Iron?

Mother finds it so easy to bake delicious light whole-some waffles on her new Heart-Star Waffle Iron that she keeps right on offering hearts, crisp and piping hot (the little stars in the center go to Peggy), until even Jimmie is filled up.

Good waffles aren't just luck. One reason why Griswold Waffle Irons turn out such tempting waffles is that the pans are uniform thickness—this distributes and holds the heat evenly, and bakes the waffles thoroughly, a beautiful even brown all over!

Notice the coil handles which are always cool, never burn out or loosen; and the ball-bearing hinge which makes it so easy to turn the pan. Cup and groove catch grease that would otherwise run down into the fire. Low rings for use on coal ranges and electric stoves and deep rings for gas and oil.

Griswold Waffle Irons make welcome gifts at all times, but this new Heart-Star design is particularly appropriate as an engagement or wedding present, and is appreciated by women who like to serve dainty dishes.

Trade Mark
Reg. U. S.
Pat. Off.

THE GRISWOLD MFG. CO.
ERIE, PENNA., U. S. A.

*Griswold Heart-Star Waffle Irons are sold in all the better stores. If your dealer hasn't them, send for our new booklet on Waffle Irons, Patty Irons and Gem Pans.*

April 1921 – Home Journal

# THE GRISWOLD BOLO OVEN

### *enables you to do more baking in less time*

THESE are the days when you want to get a lot of baking done at one time—and then stay out of the kitchen and try to keep cool!

A Bolo Oven is a special blessing just now—it means having two ovens at your disposal: one in which to do slow baking, another for fast baking!

The Griswold Bolo Oven is the only portable oven with this remarkable advantage. It's the shelf in the center, the flue plate, that makes it possible. When the oven door is shut, there are two entirely separate sections: the lower one hot for fast baking, the upper one moderately hot for slow baking. The saving of time and fuel is surprising, and especially welcome these hot days.

Bolo Ovens are light and easily moved about; and the wooden handles are always cool. The oven is made of polished steel, with double walls and nickeled steel corners; washable, non-rustable enameled top; strong hinges, rolled edges and a clamp handle make the glass door shut tight; and many special features of construction which make the Bolo both good-looking and durable.

### THE GRISWOLD MFG. CO.

ERIE, PENNA., U. S. A.

*Makers of the Bolo Oven, Extra Finished Iron Kitchen Ware, Waffle Irons, Cast Aluminum Cooking Utensils, Food Choppers, Reversible Dampers and Gas Hot Plates.*

*If your dealer does not carry Bolo Ovens, write to us and we will gladly send you our Bolo Oven Bulletin which describes and illustrates the various models.*

Trade Mark
Reg. U. S. Pat. Off.

1935 Home Journal

# MAGAZINE AD

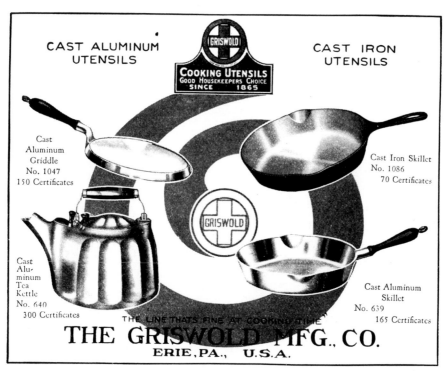

1928

# PROGRAM AD

The New Park Opera House Program from December 27, 1901.

No. 9 Tite-Top Baster with cover, p/n 834.
Marked with Griswold slant TM,
and Erie, PA, USA.
**$80**

No. 2 Scotch Bowl,
marked Erie.
**$125**

No. 3 Scotch Bowl,
p/n 781. Marked Erie.
**$125**

No. 3 Yankee Bowl, p.n 785. Marked Griswold's Erie. – **$60**
No. 3 Yankee Bowl, p/n 785. Marked
with Griswold slant TM. – **$65**

# BASTER, BOWLS, CASSEROLES, COOKERS AND POTS

No. 4 Scotch Bowl with flat bottom, p/n 839.
Marked with Griswold TM and Erie.
**$75-100**

No. 5 Scotch Bowl, p/n 783.
Marked with Griswold slant TM
and Erie. – **$125**

2 1/2 qt. Casserole and cover, p/n A152 1/2, aluminum.
Cover marked Griswold Casserole Cover pat'd Feb 10, 1920.
Erie, PA USA. – **$65 with cover**

4 pt. Casserole, p/n A184,
cast aluminum. Marked
with Griswold TM.
**$45**

No. 8 Safety Cooker, p/n 860. Marked Safety.
Made by Griswold but not marked.
**$65**

No. 8 Bulge Pot, p/n 820. Marked with
Griswold slant TM and Erie.
**$110-125**

2 3/4 qt. Pot marked
Hearthstone USA Griswold.
**$35**

No. 426 Pot and cover, 6 qt., p/n A412 and
A412C with bail/wood handle.
**$75**

# DUTCH OVENS

No. 8 Dutch Oven – 2 quart.
Marked with Griswold TM and Wagner Ware
TM also marked with an X.
**$80**

No. 10 Tite Top Dutch Oven, p/n 2553A.
Marked Griswold.
**$100**

No. 11 Dutch Oven, p/n 836 and cover p/n 2554.
Marked Erie and Griswold slant TM.
**$150**

# DUTCH OVENS

No. 8 Dutch Oven and cover. Oven is p/n 833, cover is p/n 2551A.
Both marked with Griswold slant TM and Erie.
**$60**

No. 6 Dutch Oven, p/n 2606.
Marked on lid Tite-Top Dutch
Oven, bottom marked with
Griswold TM.
**$300**

No. 8 Dutch Oven, p/n 2165.
Hammered aluminum, with glass cover.
**$75-100**

# GRIDDLES

No. 6 Griddle, p/n 506.
Marked with a Griswold TM and
Erie, PA USA.
**$125**

No. 7 Skillet handled griddle,
p/n 737. Marked with Griswold
slant TM and Erie, PA., U.S.A.
**$95**

No. 7 Rectangular Griddle,
aluminum, p/n A327.
Marked with Griswold TM.
**$75**

No. 8 Griddle (8 mark on handle) with wood handle.
**$100**

# GRIDDLES

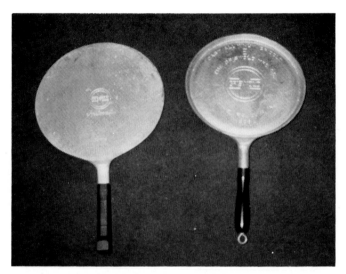

Left: No. 9 Griddle, p/n A1309 aluminum with square wood handle. Marked with Griswold TM and Aristocraft. **$75-100**

Right: No. 8 Griddle, p/n A308 aluminum with round wood handle. Marked with Griswold TM and has hang ring. **$100**

Skillet Handled Griddle, p/n 738, chrome. Marked with an Erie/ Griswold Diamond TM.
**$250**

No. 8 Handled Griddle, p/n 738.
Marked Erie.
*(Notice the difference between this Griddle and the one to the right.)*
**$100**

No. 8 Handled Griddle, p/n 738.
Marked Erie and 8.
**$75**

# GRIDDLES

No. 9 New England
Griddle.
Marked N.E. Griddle
with Griswold slant TM.
**$135**

No. 9 Long Griddle with handles, p/n 746.
Marked with Erie Diamond TM.
**$80**

No. 9 Round Handle Griddle, p/n 1508.
Marked Merit (Made by Griswold for
Sears Roebuck & Co.) Circa 1940's.
**$35**

Left to Right:

No. 10A Skillet Griddle, p/n 731.
Marked with Griswold slant TM and Erie. – **$300**

No. 7A Skillet Griddle. Marked Erie. – **$300**

No. 10 Skillet marked Erie. – **$300**

# GRIDDLES

No. 10 Handled Griddle, p/n 740.
Marked with Griswold TM.
**$95**

No. 12 Griddle with bail handle.
Marked Erie.
**$40**

No. 12 & No. 8 New England style
Griddles. Marked with Griswold slant TM.
No. 12 – **$200**     No. 8 – **$100**

No. 14 Griddle, bail handle, marked Erie.
**$65**

No. 14 Griddle, marked with a
Griswold slant TM – **$65**

# GRIDDLES

No. 16 Bail handled Griddle, p/n 743.
Marked Erie.
*(notice the next three items and how their markings differ)*
**$150**

No. 16 Bail handled Griddle, p/n 743.
Marked with Griswold slant TM and Erie.
**$190**

No. 16 Bail handled Griddle, p/n 743.
Marked with Griswold slant TM.
**$150**

No. 16 Bail handled Griddle p/n 619.
Marked with Griswold TM.
**$100**

# GRIDDLES

No. 107 Griddle, p/n 200.
Marked Cast Iron Skillet Griddle,
The Griswold Mfg., Co., Erie, PA USA
with a Griswold slant TM.
**$125**

No. 147 Gas Griddle, p/n 230.
Marked with Griswold TM.
22 7/8" long  x  13 1/4" wide
**$150**

# MUFFIN PANS

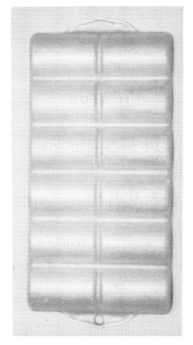

No. 11 French Roll Pan,
p/n A-8011, cast aluminum.
Marked Griswold Erie.
**$50**

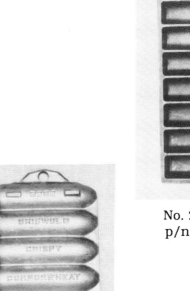

No. 22 Breadstick pan,
p/n 954. Marked Erie.
**$60**

Tea size cornstick
pan, p/n A8262.
Marked Griswold.
**$60**

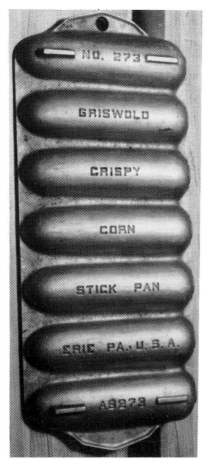

No. 273 Cornstick
Pan, aluminum,
p/n A8273. Marked
Griswold Crispy
Corn Stick Pan, Erie
PA., U.S.A.
**$70**

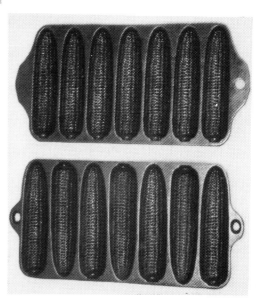

Two No. 262 Corn or Wheat Stick Pans
p/n 625.
*(Note the handles with two holes and one hole)*
**$80**

# MUFFIN PANS

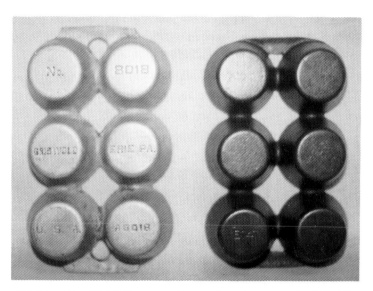

Right:  No. 8018 Popover Pan, aluminum, p/n A8018 with spiral handles. Marked Griswold, Erie, PA. – **$75**

Left:  Popover Pan, cast iron, p/n 6141 with flat handles. Marked Griswold Erie, Circa 1900. – **$80**

No. 10 Popover pan, p/n 948.
Marked Erie.
**$60**

11 Cup Muffin Pan showing when Griswold sold to Wagner. Marked with both Wagner Ware TM and Griswold TM, made in U.S.A.
**$70**

# MUFFIN PANS

No. 3 Gem Pan, p/n 942. Made by Griswold but not marked.
**$200-300**

Munk Pan, p/n 962.
Marked with an Erie Diamond TM.
**$60**

Munk Pan, p/n 2992 on handle.
Marked Alfred Anderson Munk
Pan, made by Griswold.
**$200**

# PAPER COLLECTIBLES

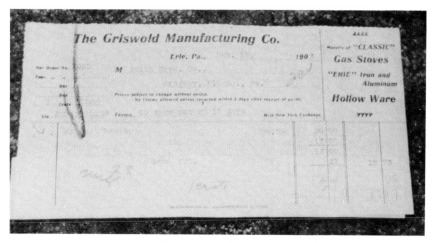

Bill of Lading from Griswold Mfg. Co, to
Smith Bros. Co. of Ridgeway, Elk County, Pennsylvania in 1903.
**$5**

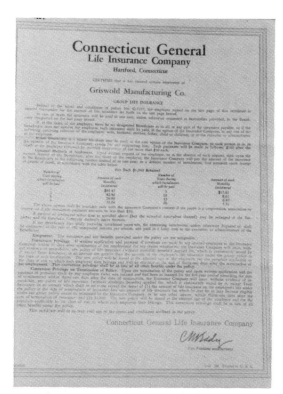

Business Card for Sears Roebuck &
Company with Griswold Mfg. Co.
on the top of the card.
**$5**

Life Insurance Company insuring
The Griswold Manufacturing
Company employees.
**$25**

# PAPER COLLECTIBLES

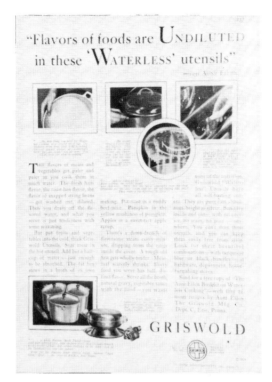

1928 Advertisement on
Waterless Utensils.
**$25**

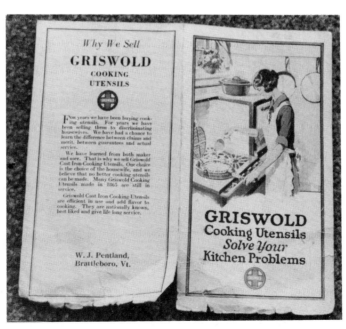

Testimonial leaflet from a Vermont Department
Store of the line of Griswold Products
that they carried.
**$10**

Deep Patty Bowls with bailed handles. Marked with Griswold TM.

No. 871 – **$75-100**     No. 72 – **$50-80**

No. 71 – **$200-250 with cover**     No. 870 Junior – **$250-350**

Aluminum Utility Bowls with wood handles and hang ring. Marked with Griswold TM.

No. 1 1/2, p/n 241 1/2 – **$150**     No. 3, p/n 343 – **$100**

No. 4, p/n 344 – **$125**     No. 5, p/n 345 – **$125**

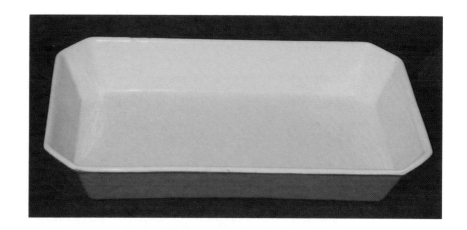

No. 81 Casserole Dish,
red & cream porcelain.
**$65-85**

Top View

Bottom View

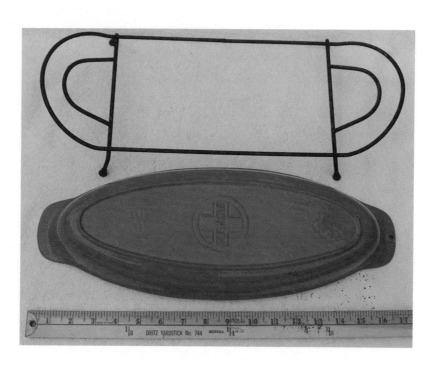

No. 82 Oval Casserole Fish
Dish with wire rack.
Marked with Griswold TM.
**with rack – $175-200**
**without rack – $75-100**

Porcelain Casserole Set with wire holder.
Marked with Griswold TM.
**$300-400**

Left: Single Service Casserole with lid, p/n 67c. Marked with Griswold TM. –**$85**
No. 0 Table Service Dutch Oven, p/n 67 with lid. Marked with Griswold TM –**$85**

No. 69 Casserole Dish with lid No. 66.
yellow porcelain with original label.
Marked with Griswold TM. –**$75-125**

Table Service Casserole with lid, p/n 845.
Marked with Griswold TM, Erie, PA, U.S.A.
**$125**

No. 8 Skillet with lid, green/white
speckled porcelain. Marked
Deep Chicken Cooker with
Griswold TM.
**$150**

No. 68 Round Casserole and Lid No. 68c,
with flared handles, Circa 1930's.
Marked with Griswold TM.
**$50**

No. 95 Oval Casserole and Lid No. 94,
with flared handles, Circa 1930's.
Marked with Griswold TM.
**$50**

No. 91 Oval Single Service Casserole.
Marked with Griswold TM.
**$75-95**

No. 89 Round Casserole Dish.
Marked with Griswold TM.
**$85-125**

No. 262 Tea Size Corn Stick Pan, p/n 625.
(with original box) Marked Griswold, Erie, PA, U.S.A.
**$150**

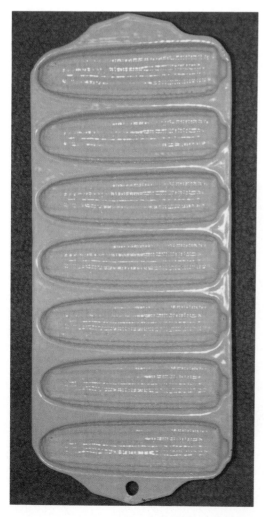

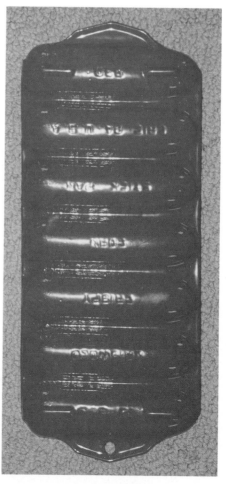

No. 273 Corn Stick Pan, p/n 930, porcelain – **$100**

No. 8 Dutch Oven, cobalt blue porcelain.
(pictured below)
**$150**

No. 8 Dutch Ovens, various enamels and chrome.
**$125-175 without trivets.**

No. 8 Hammered Aluminum Dutch Oven,
p/n 2058. Marked with Griswold TM, Erie, PA.
**$100**

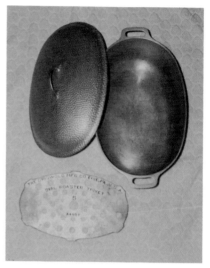

No. 5 Oval Roaster, hammered
aluminum, p/n A485 with trivet.
**$100**

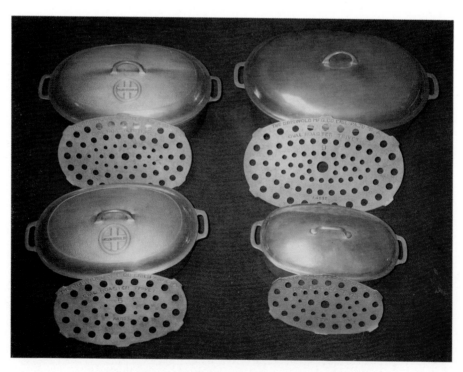

Aluminum Oval Roasters with lids and trivets.
Left to right:   No. 7, p/n A-487      No. 9, p/n A-489
No. 5, p/n A-485      No. 3, p/n A-483
**$250-350**

Original labels in skillets
**$20 each**

Skillet label
Marked "Made in America Since 1865"
"Timeless Cookware for Today's Cooks."
**$5**

No. 2 Mailbox. No pattern number.
Made by Griswold but not marked.
**$85**

No. 3 Mailbox, p/n 353, 361.
Made by Griswold but not marked.
**$85**

No. 3 Mailbox, p/n 105, 106.
Made by Griswold but not marked.
**$75**

No. 4 Post Box with p/n 354, 355, 356.
Made by Griswold but not marked.
**$45**

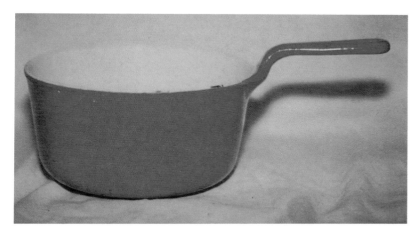

No. 84 Sauce Pan with lid, 2 quart
red and cream porcelain.
Circa 1930's.
Marked with Griswold TM.
**$150**

No. 6 Skillet
pictured in green enamel.

No. 6 Blue Skillet with Self Basting cover.
(Has original label in it.)
Marked with Griswold TM.
**$75-150**

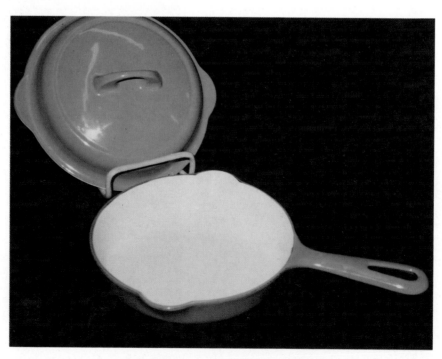

No. 3 Skillet with high domed lid.
Blue/white porcelain.
**Rare**

No. 0 Skillet, porcelain, p/n 562.
Marked with Griswold TM
**$75**

Skillet p/n 2705 has a white enamel inside.
Marked with a Griswold TM.
**$65-100**

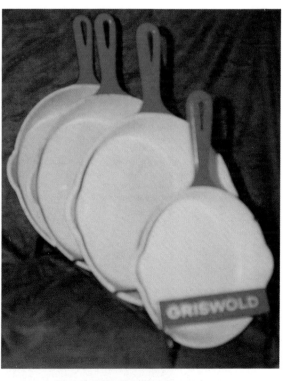

Wire Skillet Rack – **$200**
No.'s 8, 7, 6, 3 porcelain skillets shown
Marked with Griswold TM on bottom.
**$25 each skillet**

No. 8 Skillet chromed, p/n 715
with lid p/n 1098B. Cast in 1930's.
Marked Griswold under handle.
**$175**

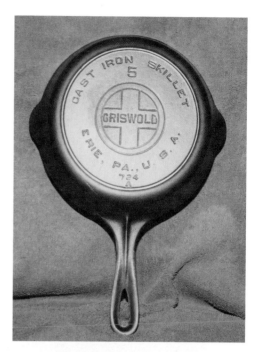

No. 5 Skillet, aluminum
with smoke ring, p/n 724A.
Marked with Griswold TM.
**Rare**

No. 9 Hammered Griddle, p/n 2039.
Marked with Griswold TM, Erie PA.
**$75**

No. 5 Hammered Skillet, p/n 2015
with lid. Marked with Griswold TM, Erie, PA.
**$125**

8 inch Deep Skillet, symbol aluminum
#95, with bakelite handle.
**$10**

Deep skillet and lid, aluminum p/n A128 and cover p/n A1208C.
Marked with Griswold TM and Aristocraft Ware.
**$65**

4 Coffee Grinders, all identical
but in varying degrees of restoration.
All marked Griswold Mfg. Company.
**$1000 in fine condition**

Tea Kettles, all are cast aluminum
with wood handle grips.
Tea Kettle #A-51 – **$200**    No. 4 Tea Kettle – **$100**
No. 505 Tea Kettle, 5 qt. – **$30**

No. 4 Chromed Tea Kettle with wood handle.
Marked Erie
**$100**

Brass Erie Kettle with
wire handle.
**$100**

Coffee Pots, aluminum. One with and one without
drip section and strainer, p/n 1602.
Marked Aristocraft with Griswold TM.
**$150 complete**
**$75 without insides**

No. A1534 Aluminum Tea Kettle
(5 quart). Marked Aristocraft Ware.
**$50**

No. 8 Waffle Iron pans, p/n 395.
Marked Victor, made by Griswold.
**$45**

No. 8 American Waffle Iron, p/n 886.
Marked with Griswold TM on one side,
and Puritan on reverse side.
**$85-100**

No. 8 Hammered Waffle Iron
Marked with Griswold TM.
**$275**

No.'s 10, 11, 12, and 13 Grinders, all marked Puritan.
The handles are marked The Griswold Mfg., Co., Erie, PA USA
**$25 each**
From the collection of Bob Chandler

No. 2 Fruit and Lard Press – 4qt., p/n 2610 bottom, p/n 2611 cross bar.
Marked on bottom with Griswold slant TM.
**$150**
From the collection of Bob Chandler

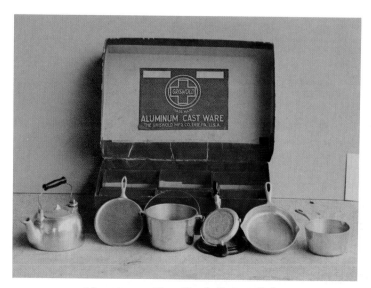

Aluminum Toy Cook Set with box
**Rare**

Sauce Pans and covers, hammered aluminum
with wood handle and hang ring.
No. 2141 – 1 quart
No. 2142 – 2 quart
No. 2144 – 4 quart
**$75 each**

Deep Fat Fryer with wire basket, p/n 1003.
Marked with Griswold TM.
**$100-150**

Coal and/or Wood Oven
p/n 125.
16 9/16" high x 13 1/4" wide x 12 1/2" deep.
Marked with Griswold TM.
**$100**

Cast Iron Stove, marked
Eriez Stove & Mfg. Co.
Made in Erie, PA
**$200**

Two step stool in cast chrome with
rubber treads. Marked Griswold.
**$200**

Combination Bar Stool and two step
stool that tucks away for storage
underneath the bar stool.
**$300**

Griswold Mfg. Company Employees
Bowling League Banquet Program for 1954,
and two trophies and bowling patch for 1954.
**program – $30**
**patch – $20**
**trophies – Rare**

A view of some of the collection of Bill and Lynda Cervenka.

Dick and Esther Miller pictured here with some of their collection.

These two groups of porcelain pieces
are from the collection of
Dr. Joseph A. Noto, M.D.

Red set includes: round and oval casseroles,
fish dishes, ash trays, sauce pot with lid,
corn stick pan, no. 18 griddle - **All $150 each**
and skillets in a rack with labels – **$50**

Below: the yellow set includes:
round, square, and oval casseroles; ashtrays;
no. 0 skillet – **All $150 each**
and no.'s 4,5,6,7 skillets – **$50 each.**

Porcelain pieces from the collection of Nancy Lee Brown
No. 0 Skillet with smoke ring, p/n 562. Marked with Griswold TM.
No. 0 Table Service Dutch Oven, p/n 67 and cover p/n 67c. Marked with Griswold TM.
No. 95 Oval Casserole dish with lid no. 94. Marked with Griswold TM.

Cast Aluminum pieces from the collection of Nancy Lee Brown
8 qt. Colonial Design Tea Kettle, p/n A358A. Marked with Griswold TM.
2 qt. Sauce Pan with wood handles, p/n 412. Marked with Griswold TM.
No. 8 Drip Drop Roaster, p/n 248. Marked with Wagner Ware TM.

Griswold Tote Grill, p/n 137. Made by Randall Mfg. after 1957 – **$70**

No. 15 Oval Skillet p/n 1013, with matching cover p/n 1013c.
This set is Rare – **$800**
From the collection of Craig Leverenz
(Pictured is Baron "Dusty Bunny" Von Griswold now 14 months old exploring the skillet)

Griswold Factory Time Clock.
Has Griswold TM and The Griswold Mfg. Co.
on the face of the clock. (one-of-a-kind)
Made by Bulova.
**Rare**
From the collection of Joseph A. Noto, MD

A full set of hammered black cast iron ware made by Griswold. All that have lids are hinged.
From the collection of Joseph A. Noto, MD

From the collection of Larry and Sue Foxx

From the collection of Robert F. Petty

A collection of porcelain skillets.

These pictures are from the collection of
Robert & Doris Mosier.

A collection of all different items that they have collected through the years.

Griswold cast iron skillet with Mercedes the cat
lounging in the skillet owned by Rita Densham.

From the collection of Gary and Charline Wineteer.

Two views of some of the cast iron and porcelain collection of Craig Leverenz

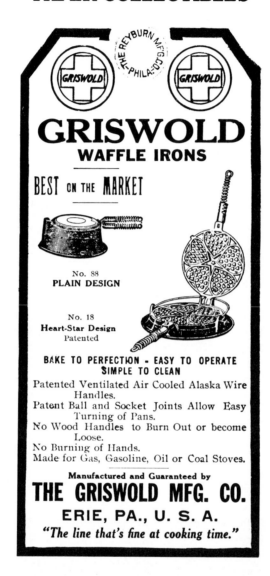

## CRISP GOLDEN BROWN WAFFLES
### HOW TO PREPARE A WAFFLE IRON FOR USE

Place iron over low fire and grease inside of pan thoroughly several times (use brush for best results.) Allow iron to remain over fire until pan has thoroughly absorbed the grease. Repeat grease operation and the iron is ready for use.

**IN BAKING WAFFLES,** place iron over fire, and grease inside of pan with clean lard. When iron is thoroughly heated pour batter in center of pan, using spoon or ladle large enough to hold batter to fill pan. Close pan, bake on one side, turn and bake on the other side. Raise upper half and remove waffle with a fork. The first waffle in a new pan may stick, but as soon as pan has absorbed the grease and becomes hot enough, there will be no further trouble.

**NOTE.**—Do not wash pan. Scrape burnt grease and batter off with knife. Place pan in paper bag to keep clean when not in use.

### WAFFLE RECIPE

**NO. 1.**—2 cups milk, 2 eggs, 3 cups flour, 1 teaspoonful cream of tartar, ½ teaspoonful soda, 1 salt-spoonful salt, 1 tablespoonful melted butter, sift the cream of tartar into the flour with salt, dissolve the soda in a little hot water, beat the eggs very well, add the flour the last thing. If the batter is too stiff, put in more milk.

**NO. 2**—Beat 3 eggs, mix well 1 quart of sifted flour with 3 teaspoonfuls of baking powder dry, rub ½ of a cupful of butter into the flour and then add the eggs. Use milk enough to make a batter which will pour into WAFFLE PAN, filling it two-thirds full.

### ECONOMY WAFFLES

**NO. 3**—1 cup of rice flour, 1 cup of corn flour, 1 teaspoonful salt, 1 teaspoonful sugar, 4 teaspoonfuls baking powder, 2 cups milk, 3 tablespoonfuls fat, 2 eggs. Use level measurements and sift the flour once before measuring. Sift the flour, salt, baking powder and sugar together, and stir into them the milk. Separate the eggs, and beat the yolks into the mixture. Melt the fat and add it. When mixed thoroughly, beat the egg whites stiff and fold them into the batter. Sufficient for five waffles.

Griswold Waffle Iron Tag – original
(front and back view)
**$60**

# PAPER COLLECTIBLES

Postcard depicting the new Post Office in the
Griswold Plaza in Erie, PA, dedicated
December 1, 1932 at a cost of $500,000.
The message by the sender was "This is our
new post office. It is opposite the new depot.
It is grand inside, I went to the dedication.
(Postage in 1932 was 1 1/2 cent if you had
no message, and just a signature or
message is 3 cents.
**Rare**

Picture of the inside of the Griswold Manufacturing Company.
Showing the men and women at work.
**Rare**

Cast Aluminum Cooking Utensils Catalog.
June 29, 1928 – **$145-175**

Aunt Ellen's Dutch Oven Dishes
Recipe Booklet © 1927 – **$100-150**

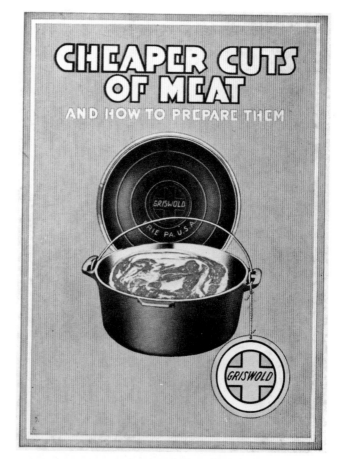

Cheaper Cuts of Meat and How To Prepare Them
Recipe Booklet © 1919. – **$145-175**

# PATTY MOLDS

Complete set of Patty Molds with
cooking pot and four molds.
**$125**

Two different sets of Patty Molds, left set is shallow, right set is deep.
**$40 each set**

# PLATTERS AND PLATES

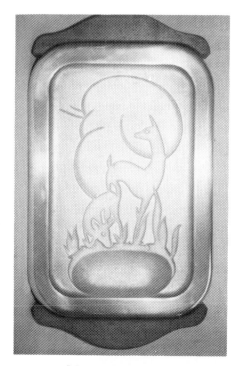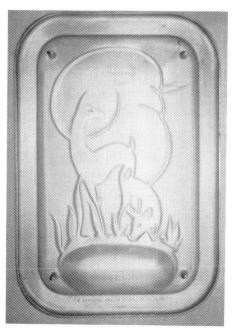

Meat or Venison Platter with wooden holder, p/n A2082.
Cast aluminum. Marked Aristocraft Ware
with Griswold TM.
**$75**

Family Tree Platter, p/n A2191.
Cast aluminum, marked Griswold.
**$65**

# PLATTERS AND PLATES

8 inch Steak Plate, p/n 1056.
Marked with Griswold TM and
The Griswold Mfg., Co., Erie, PA, U.S.A.
**$50**

Steak Platter, p/n 848, c. 1940.
(This piece may have been stripped as most Steak Platters
seem to have been made in chrome plate finish.)
Marked with Griswold TM, Erie, PA., U.S.A.
**$50**

# PLATTERS AND PLATES

7 1/2 inch Hot Service Plate,
p/n 855. Marked with
Griswold TM, Erie, PA., U.S.A.
**$125**

9 inch Hot Service Plate, p/n 850.
Marked with Griswold TM,
Erie, PA., U.S.A.
**$150**

Oval Tree Platter, p/n 861.
Marked Griswold Tree Platter, Erie, PA., U.S.A.
**$175**

# ROASTERS

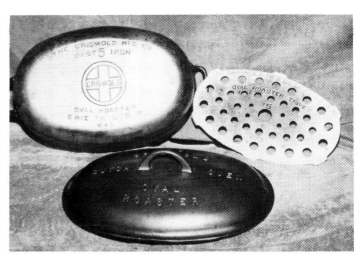

No. 5 Oval Roaster, hammered aluminum,
p/n 2185. Marked with Griswold TM.
**$150 without trivet**

No. 5 Oval Roaster with trivet, p/n 645.
Marked with Griswold TM on bottom, cover
marked Griswold and trivet marked Griswold.
**$450**

No. 5 Oval Roaster with cover, p/n 2629 and cover p/n 2630.
Marked with Griswold slant TM.
**$500**

No. 5 Oval Roaster with cover and
trivet, p/n A1485.
Marked with Griswold TM and
Aristocraft. – **$75-100**

# ROASTERS

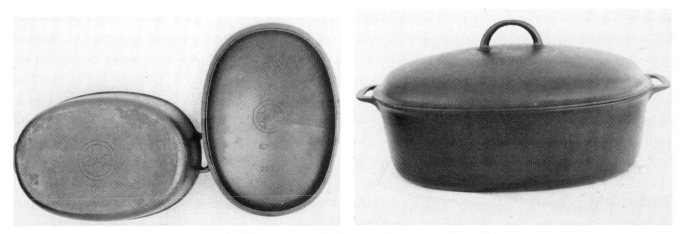

No. 7 Oval Roaster p/n 2631 with cover p/n 2632.
Both marked with Griswold slant TM and Erie.
**$200**

Stamped aluminum trivet for
Dutch Oven, 8 inch diameter.
Griswold name stamped on it.
**$20**

No. 7 Oval Roaster p/n 487, cover p/n A487C,
and trivet p/n A487T, aluminum.
**$200**

# SAUCEPAN

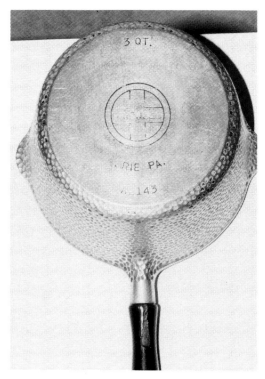

Bottom view of 3 qt. Saucepan,
p/n A2143, hammered aluminum.
Marked with Griswold TM and Erie.
**$35**

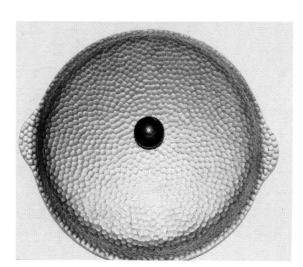 

3 qt. Saucepan Cover, view of top and inside cover,
p/n 2143C. The cover has basting rings and Marked Griswold inside.
**$20**

# SAUCEPANS

1 pint Aluminum Nursery Saucepan with
alcohol lamp, p/n 41. Black wooden handle
with original box. Marked Erie.
**Rare**

No. A702 Double Boiler, 2 quart.
Top pan and cover is pressed aluminum.
Bottom pan is cast aluminum.
**$55**

4 quart Saucepan, cast aluminum, p/n 434.
Marked with Griswold TM.
**$35**

Aluminum Saucepans, square handles,
with covers. All marked Aristocraft.
*(L to R)* p/n A1511, p/n 1512, and p/n 1513.
**$75 each with cover**

# SKILLET COVERS

No. 8 Aluminum Skillet Cover, p/n A208C.
Marked with Griswold TM, Pat'd Sept. 22, 1925
**$25**

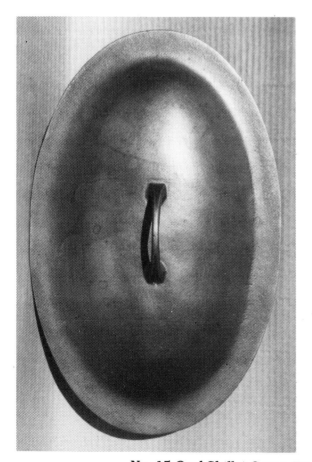

No. 15 Oval Skillet Cover. Fits a 15 x 10 pan, p/n 1013C.
Circa 1930's. Marked Self Basting with Griswold TM – **$750  (rare)**

# SKILLET COVERS

No. 5 Skillet cover, p/n 1095.
Marked Self Basting with Griswold TM.
**$70**

No. 7 Skillet cover, p/n 467.
Marked Griswold Self Basting
Skillet Cover.
**$60**

No. 12 Skillet cover, no pattern number.
Marked Griswold Self Basting
Skillet Cover.
**$100**

Washington Bicentennial Cover,
Chrome plated.
Marked Washington Bi-Centennial 1732-1932.
**$350-400**

# SKILLETS

*(Skillets are arranged according to their Trademarks)*

*(L to R)* No. 6 Skillet with smoke ring, p/n 699B.
Marked Griswold's Erie. – **$50**

No. 9 Skillet with smoke ring, p/n 710A.
Marked Erie – **$70**

No. 7 Skillet, p/n 701F.
Marked Erie.
**$40**

No. 8 Skillet p/n 704.
Marked Erie.
*(Note different p/n on the picture at the right)*
**$40**

No. 8 Deep Skillet, p/n 732.
Marked Erie.
**$85**

# SKILLETS

No. 8A Shallow Skillet, p/n 729.
Marked Erie with three holes in handle.
**$95**

No. 9 Skillet with heat ring,
p/n 710A. Marked Erie.
**$70**

No. 10 Skillet with heat ring,
p/n 715. Marked Erie.
**$60**

No. 10 Skillet, no pattern number.
Marked Erie.
**$75**

# SKILLETS

No. 12 Skillet with heat ring.
Marked Erie.
**$125**

No. 4 Skillet, p/n 702.
Marked with Griswold
slant TM and Erie.
**$75**

No. 7 Skillet, p/n 701.
Marked with Griswold slant
TM and Erie.
**$45**

No. 7 Skillet, p/n 701A.
Marked Griswold's Erie.
**$55**

# SKILLETS

No. 8 Skillet, p/n 704D.
Marked with Griswold
slant TM and Erie.
**$40**

No. 9 Skillet with wood handle,
p/n 727. Marked with Griswold
slant TM and Erie.
**$85**

No. 0 Chrome Skillet,
p/n 562. 4 3/8" dia.,
with early handle,
circa 1930's. Marked
Griswold Erie PA U.S.A.
**$75**

No. 6 Skillet and cover, p/n 2106.
Hammered aluminum. – **$75**

No. 8 Skillet, p/n 2108.
Hammered aluminum. – **$75**

# SKILLETS

No. 11 Skillet, p/n 372 and No. 12 Skillet, p/n 373.
Both marked with Griswold slant TM, Erie PA USA.
**No. 11 – $300-400    No. 12 – $200-300**

No. 14 Bailed handle skillet, p/n 694.
Marked with Griswold TM, Erie PA USA.
**$600-800**

No. 20 Skillet with smoke ring, p/n 728.
The skillet has two handles and is marked
with a Griswold TM, Erie PA USA.
**$550**

# SKILLETS

No. 8 Skillet and cover, chromed, p/n 715.
The smooth flat bottom has no markings,
the p/n is marked under the handle.
The cover is marked with Griswold TM.
**Rare**

No. 4 Skillet unusual top edge that is
thicker than most skillets, 2 1/8" diameter.
Marked with Griswold TM and 7 inch skillet.
**Rare**

No. 12 Skillet, p/n 719B.
Marked with Griswold TM.
**$85**

# SKILLETS

No. 42 Snack Skillet.
Marked with Griswold TM.
**$85**

Skillet p/n 2705,
with white enamel inside.
Marked with Griswold TM.
**$65-100**

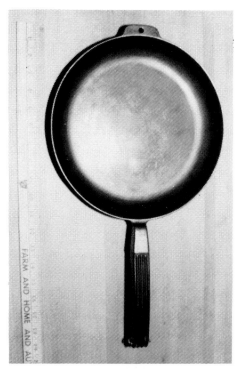

Skillet p/n 2703 with bakelite handle.
Marked with Griswold TM.
**$50-75**

# SKILLETS

Aluminum Skillet with covers and wood handles.
*(L to R)*   p/n A1206 – **$75**      p/n 1208 – **$75**
p/n 128 – **$100**

No. 43 Chef Skillet, 9 inches. Circa early 1950's.
Marked with Griswold TM. – **$35**

No. 0 Chef Skillet, circa late 1950's.
Marked with Griswold TM and Wagner Ware TM. – **$35**

# SKILLETS

7 3/4 inch Skillet, cast iron.
Circa late 1950's.
Marked Hearthstone-Griswold.
**$25**

No. 8 Good Health Skillet, p/n 658.
Made by Griswold.
**$25**

No. 8 Skillet, p/n 755. (similar to
Victor) Made by Griswold, not marked.
**$25**

# SKILLETS

No. 5 Skillet, p/n 635.
Marked The Last Iron Skillet
The Griswold Mfg. Co, Erie, PA, U.S.A.
**$400**

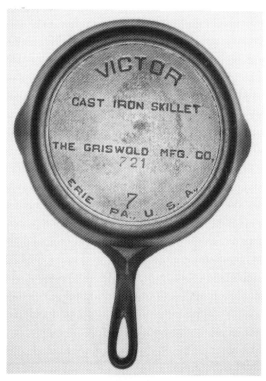

No. 7 Skillet, p/n 721.
Marked Victor, Griswold Mfg. Co.
**$60**

No. 8 Skillet, p/n 722A.
Marked Victor and The Griswold Mfg., Co,
Erie, PA, U.S.A.
**$50**

# TEA KETTLES

No. 5 Tea Kettle, p/n 6806. Marked Erie.
**$80**

No. 8 Tea Kettle (5 quart), p/n 506.
Marked Griswold's Erie Rapid.
**$80**

# TEA KETTLES

2 quart Tea Kettle, p/n AA-516.
Marked Griswold slant TM.
**$50**

2 quart Tea Kettle, cast aluminum, p/n 532.
Marked Colonial Design with Griswold slant TM and Erie PA., U.S.A.
**$40**

# TEA KETTLES

5 quart Tea Kettle, hammered
aluminum, p/n A2135.
Marked with Griswold TM,
Erie PA., U.S.A.
**$50**

*(L to R)* 5 quart Tea Kettle with ripple bottom – **$75-100**

2 quart Tea Kettle, p/n 512. Marked with Griswold TM. – **$75-100**

2 pint Tea Kettle, p/n 133. Marked with Griswold TM. – **$75-100**

No. 123 Coffee Pot (3 pint),
cast aluminum.
**$85**

Coffee Pots *(L to R)*
No. 1713 – **$100**

No. A-16 with base separator
– **$100**

No. A-105 with base
separator – **$100**

No. A-134 (4 pint) Perculator
with Griswold TM – **$100**

# WAFFLE IRONS

No. 7 Waffle Iron, p/n 966, 973, base 972.
Marked Griswold Mfg., Co., Erie PA. The New American marked in middle.
**$125**

No. 8 Waffle Iron, no pattern number.
Marked The American, Griswold
Mfg. Co., Erie PA.
American marked in middle.
**$100**

No. 8 Waffle Iron, p/n 151N,
base p/n 152. Marked
The Griswold Mfg., Co., Erie PA., USA,
and marked American.
**$65**

# WAFFLE IRONS

No. 8 Waffle Iron, p/n 885, 886
and base p/n 975. Marked American,
The Griswold Mfg., Co., Erie PA., U.S.A.
with Griswold slant TM.
**$85**

No. 8 Waffle Iron with high base,
p/n 976, 977 and base has no p/n.
Marked The Griswold Mfg. Co., The
New American, Erie PA, U.S.A.
**$85**

No. 9 Waffle Iron, p/n 980, 979, base
978. Marked with Griswold slant TM
and American.
**$100**

No. 628 Waffle Iron, base p/n 152.
Marked with Griswold TM,
American, The Griswold Mfg., Co.
**$50**

# WAFFLE IRONS

No. 18 Heart and Star, p/n 919.
Marked Griswold slant TM, Erie PA., U.S.A.
**$150**

No. 18 Heart and Star Waffle Iron.
**$175**

# WAFFLE IRONS

No. 12 Waffle Iron with wood handles,
p/n 2608. Marked with Griswold slant TM.
**$600**

No. 8 Waffle Iron, p/n 395.
Marked Good Health.
Made by Griswold.
**$75**

Heart shaped Waffle Iron.
Marked Alfred Andersen & Co., Minneapolis
and marked Heart Shaped Design.
**$145**

# WAFFLE IRONS

No. 8 Waffle Iron, p/n 983 and 984.
Marked Griswold Mfg., Co., Erie, PA
and Victor marked in the middle.
**$125**

No. 8 Waffle Iron, p/n 328, 333, 314.
Marked Puritan and
base marked Griswold.
**$55**

No. 8 Waffle Iron, p/n 885, 886 and
base p/n 975. Marked Puritan
and base marked Griswold.
**$55**

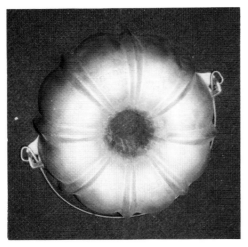

Bundt Pan, aluminum, p/n A65
with bail handle. Marked
Cake Mold, The Griswold Mfg., Co.,
Erie, PA., U.S.A.
**$250-300**

Cuspidor 11 1/2" dia. x 7 1/2" high.
Marked Selden & Griswold, Erie, PA.
**Rare**

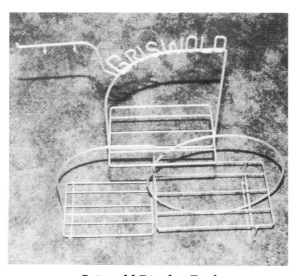

Griswold Display Rack
**Rare**

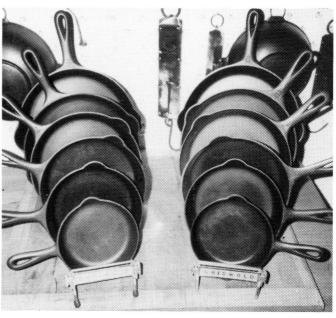

Griswold Store Skillet Display Rack.
**$300**

# MISCELLANEOUS

Fluter 5 3/4" x 3 1/8", nickel plated
cast iron. Marked The Erie Fluter.
**$675**

No. 1 Food Chopper.
Marked Griswold
Mfg. Co., Erie, PA.
**$45**

Commerical Waterless Warmer and
instructions with original box.
**$300-400**

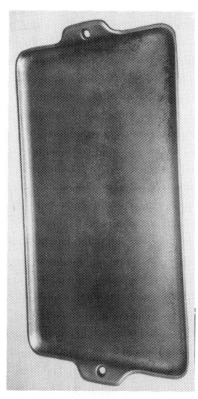

Grill, cast iron, c. 1935.
Marked Griswold.
**$100**

# MISCELLANEOUS

No. 118A Grill/Cookie Sheet, cast aluminum.
Marked Griswold Mfg., Co., Erie, PA,., U.S.A.
Also marked with Griswold TM, Since 1865,
Griswold Aristocraft All Purpose Grill.
**$50**

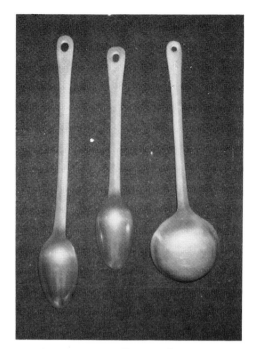

Aluminum Ladles and spoons.
Marked Griswold.
**$50 each**

6 quart Milk Box.
Marked with Griswold TM.
**$300-600**

No. 564 Lard Ladle,
cast aluminum. Marked
with Griswold TM.
**$30**

# MISCELLANEOUS

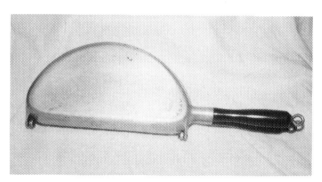

No. A54R and A54L Omelet Pan,
cast aluminum. Marked with Griswold TM.
**$65**

Rarebit Dish, p/n 1528.
Marked with Griswold TM,
Erie, PA., U.S.A.
**$85**

Printers Block or cut.
Skillet **$300**
Trademark **$400**

# MISCELLANEOUS

Sad Iron Heater, p/n 1313, c. early
1900's-1930. Marked The Griswold Mfg.,
Co., Erie, PA., Classic, Sad Iron Heater.
**$125**

No. 7 Sad Iron Heater or Long Pan.
Deep Style. – **$100-125**

Single Stove with simmer burner, p/n 401.
**$75**

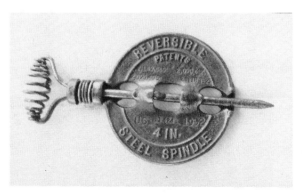

4 inch Stove Damper, p/n 1424.
Marked Griswold, Erie, PA., U.S.A.
(Note US and dated 1952)
**$35**

# MISCELLANEOUS

Tobacco Cutter Advertising "Piper-Heidsieck".
Unusual two color pinstrings (gold & red).
Manufactured by Griswold Mfg., Co., Erie, PA.
**$250**

Toy Cookware Set. Advertisement by Griswold featuring
Mother/Daughter set for sale for $4.95. This set features:
No. 775 Toy Skillet - square, a No. 262 Tea Size Corn
Stick Pan, a No. 0 Dutch Oven, and a No. 0 Round Skillet.
Ad – **$25**     Toy Set – **$600**

# PATTERN NUMBERS
## of the Griswold Manufacturing Company,
## Erie, Pennsylvania
## 1865-1957
### Compiled By Steve Stephens

| P/N | NO. | ITEM | Other Information |
|-----|-----|------|-------------------|
| 30 | | Griswold Pup | |
| 32 | | Wind Proof Ash Tray | smaller than p/n 33 |
| 33 | | Wind Proof Ash Tray | |
| 40 | 2 | Base for fruit and lard press | |
| 41 | 2 | Strainer Plate for fruit and lard press | |
| 42 | 2 | Plunger Plate for fruit and lard press | |
| 43 | 2 | Cross Bar for fruit and lard press | |
| 45 | 2 | Lever Handle for fruit and lard press | |
| 47 | 4 | Base for fruit and lard press | |
| 48 | 4 | Strainer Plate for fruit and lard press | |
| 49 | 4 | Plunger Plate for fruit and lard press | |
| 50 | 4 | Cross Bar for fruit and lard press | |
| 52 | 4 & 6 | Lever Handle for fruit and lard press | |
| 54 | 10 | Base for fruit and lard press | |
| 55 | 10 | Strainer Plate for fruit and lard press | |
| 56 | 10 | Plunger Plate for fruit and lard press | |
| 57 | 10 | Cross Bar for fruit and lard press | |
| 59 | 10 | Lever Handle for fruit and lard press | |
| 63 | | Table Service Pot | |
| 67 | 0 | Casserole Dish | cover is p/n 67C |
| 68 | | Cover for Casserole Dish | see p/n 69 |
| 69 | | Casserole Dish | cover is p/n 68 |
| 71 | | Deep Patty Bowl | smaller than p/n 72 |
| 72 | | Deep Patty Bowl | larger than p/n 71 |
| 77 | 6 | Base for fruit and lard press | |
| 78 | 6 | Strainer Plate for fruit and lard press | |
| 79 | 6 | Plunger Plate for fruit and lard press | |
| 80 | 6 | Cross Bar for fruit and lard press | |
| 82 | | Oval Service Dish | |
| 83 | | Service Casserole Dish | |
| 84 | | Sauce Pan | |
| 87 | | Fish Service Dish | |
| 89 | | Casserole Dish | |
| 91 | | Oval Casserole Dish | cover is p/n 91C |
| 93 | | Oval Bean Pot | cover is p/n 93C |
| 100 | 110 | Base for fruit and lard press | |
| 101 | 110 | Strainer Plate for fruit and lard press | |
| 102 | 110 | Plunger Plate for fruit and lard press | |
| 103 | 110 | Cross Bar for fruit and lard press | |
| 104 | 110 | Lever Handle for fruit and lard press | |
| 105 | | Mailbox Top Flap | |
| 106 | | Mailbox Top | |
| 107 | 3 | Mailbox Body | c. 1940's |
| 109 | 0 | Table Service Dutch Oven | cover is p/n 581 |
| 111 | 603 | 3 PT Casserole | |
| 112 | | Casserole Lid for p/n 111 | |
| 123 | | 3 pt. Coffee Pot – aluminum | |
| 125 | | Coal and/or Wood Oven | |
| 128 | | Skillet with cover and wood handle – aluminum | |
| 129 | | Square Egg Skillet | |
| 133 | | 2 pt. Tea Kettle | |
| 135 | 201 | Ring surrounding valve at end of burner on gas hot plate | |
| 141 | 6 | Waffle Iron | 1922 patent & later |
| 142 | 6 | Waffle frame, low, bailed handle | for p/n 141 irons |
| 143 | 6 | Waffle frame, low, side handles | for p/n 141 irons |

| P/N | NO. | ITEM | Other Information |
|---|---|---|---|
| 146 | 7 | Waffle Iron | 1922 patent & later |
| 147 | 7 | Waffle frame, low, bailed handle | for p/n 146 irons |
| 148 | 77 | Waffle frame, high, bailed handle | for p/n 146 irons |
| 149 | 7 | Waffle frame, low, side handles | for p/n 146 irons |
| 150 | 77 | Waffle frame, high, side handles | for p/n 146 irons |
| 151 | 8 | Waffle Iron | 1922 patent or later |
| 152 | 8 | Waffle frame, low, bailed handle | for p/n 151 irons |
| 153 | 88 | Waffle frame, high, bailed handle | for p/n 151 irons |
| 154 | 8 | Waffle frame, low, side handles | for p/n 151 irons |
| 155 | 88 | Waffle frame, high, side handles | for p/n 151 irons |
| 156 | 9 | Waffle Iron | 1922 patent or later |
| 157 | 9 | Waffle frame, low, bailed handle | for p/n 156 irons |
| 158 | 99 | Waffle frame, high, bailed handle | for p/n 156 irons |
| 159 | 9 | Waffle frame, low, side handles | for p/n 156 irons |
| 160 | 99 | Waffle frame, high, side handles | for p/n 156 irons |
| 161 | 11 | Square Waffle Iron | 1922 patent or later |
| 162 | 111 | Square Waffle frame, low, bailed handle | for p/n 161 irons |
| 164 | | Waffle Iron, rectangular, 3-section | fits p/n 166 & frames 12 & 14 |
| 166 | 13 | Waffle frame, rectangular | uses three p/n 164 irons |
| 171 | 8 | Waffle Iron, hammered surface | has bakelite handle |
| 172 | 8 | Waffle Iron, hammered surface | has bakelite handle |
| 173 | 8 | Waffle frame, low, side handles, hammered | for p/n 171 & 172 irons |
| 180 | 10 | Dutch Oven, bailed, with legs | uses cover p/n 843, see *310 |
| 185 | 201 | Gas Hot Plate, one burner | see p/n 191 & 1834 |
| 187 | 203 | Gas Hot Plate, three burners | see p/n 191 & 1834 |
| 188 | 8 | Trivet for dutch oven , not marked Griswold | |
| 189 | 9 | PURITAN Dutch Oven Trivet (made by Sears) | see p/n 479 |
| 191 | | Burner for gas hot plate Nos. 201 & 203 | see p/n 187 |
| 200 | 107 | Skillet Griddle | |
| 201 | 108 | Skillet Griddle | |
| 202 | 109 | Skillet Griddle | |
| 203 | 110 | Skillet Griddle | |
| 204 | 6 | Dutch Oven Trivet | |
| 205 | 7 | Dutch Oven Trivet | |
| 206 | 8 | Dutch Oven Trivet | |
| 207 | 9 | Dutch Oven Trivet | |
| 208 | 10 | Dutch Oven Trivet | |
| 209 | 11 | Dutch Oven Trivet | |
| 210 | 12 | Dutch Oven Trivet | |
| 211 | 13 | Dutch Oven Trivet | |
| 212 | | Sausage Griddle for use on commercial stove Nos. 150-160 | |
| 218 | 3 | Oval Roaster Trivet | see p/n 274 |
| 230 | 147 | Gas Griddle | |
| 233 | 150-160 | Grate for use on commercial stove Nos. 150-160 | |
| 234 | 8 | Waffle Iron, CLOWS in pattern (both irons are same p/n) | |
| 235 | 8 | Waffle frame, low, bailed, for CLOWS irons | |
| 236 | 9 | Waffle Iron, CLOWS in pattern (both irons are same p/n) | |
| 237 | 9 | Waffle frame, low, bailed, for CLOWS irons | |
| 238 | | Left & Right Small pieces to clamp wire supports on 5-tier Dutch Oven Rack | |
| 239 | | Small feet for 5-tier Dutch Oven Rack (1069) | |
| 241 1/2 | 1 1/2 | Utility bowl w/wood handle | |
| 257 | 1 | Classic Ice Shave body | |
| 258 | 1 | Classic Ice Shave top | |
| 259 | | Classic Ice Shave, piece that clamps blade | |
| 274 | 3 | Oval Roaster Trivet | |
| 275 | 5 | Oval Roaster Trivet | see p/n 218 |
| 276 | 7 | Oval Roaster Trivet | |
| 277 | 9 | Oval Roaster Trivet | |
| 297 | | The Erie Fluter fluting iron, bottom | |
| 298 | | The Erie Fluter fluting iron, top | |
| 299 | | Skillet Grill | fits in size 8 skillet |
| 300 | | Heat Regulator | |

| P/N | NO. | ITEM | Other Information |
|-----|-----|------|-------------------|
| 301 | 8 | Stove Lid Lifter | |
| 305 | 6 | Waffle Iron | note: 1908 patent on all irons through 317-331 & 336 |
| 306 | 6 | Waffle Iron | |
| 307 | 6 | Waffle frame, low, bailed handle | for irons p/n 305 & 306 |
| 308 | 7 | Waffle Iron | |
| 309 | 7 | Waffle Iron | |
| 310 | 7 | Waffle frame, low, bailed handle | for irons p/n 308 & 309 |
| 311 | 7 | Waffle frame, high, bailed handle | for irons p/n 308 & 309 |
| 312 | 8 | Waffle Iron | p/n 312 & 313 appear identical to p/n 314 & 315 |
| 313 | 8 | Waffle Iron | |
| 314 | 8 | Waffle Iron | see above |
| 315 | 8 | Waffle Iron | |
| 316 | 9 | Waffle Iron | |
| 317 | 9 | Waffle Iron | |
| 318 | 9 | Waffle frame, low, bailed handle | for irons p/n 316 & 317 or 932 & 933 |
| 319 | 9 | Waffle frame, high, bailed handle | for irons p/n 316 & 317 or 932 & 933 |
| 320 | 8 | Waffle ring for use on stoves Nos. 150-160 | for irons p/n 314 & 315 or 919 & 920 |
| 321 | 9 | Waffle ring for use on stoves Nos. 150-160 | for irons p/n 316 & 317 or 932 & 933 |
| 322 | 111 | Square Waffle frame, low | for irons p/n 363 & 364, see 162 |
| 324 | 6 | Waffle frame, low, side handles | for irons p/n 305 & 306 |
| 325 | 7 | Waffle frame, low, side handles | for irons p/n 308 & 309 |
| 326 | 7 | Waffle frame, high, side handles | for irons p/n 308 & 309 |
| 327 | 8 | Waffle frame, low, side handles | for irons p/n 314 & 315 or 919 & 920 |
| 328 | 8 | Waffle frame, high, side handles | for irons p/n 314 & 315 or 919 & 920 |
| 329 | 9 | Waffle frame, low, side handles | for irons p/n 316 & 317 or 932 & 933 |
| 330 | 9 | Waffle frame, high, side handles | for irons p/n 316 & 317 or 932 & 933 |
| 331 | 8 | Waffle Iron, not marked Griswold | other half is p/n 336; patent 1908 |
| 333 | 8 | Waffle Iron, marked PURITAN (female ball joint) | PURITAN is a Sears Trademark |
| 334 | 8 | Waffle Iron, marked Rav-O-Noc, H.S.B & Co. | frame p/n 884 |
| 335 | 8 | Waffle Iron, marked Rav-O-Noc, H.S.B & Co. | frame p/n 884 |
| 336 | 8 | Waffle Iron, not marked Griswold | other half is p/n 331; patent 1908 |
| 339 | 8 | Waffle frame, low, no handle, unusual | |
| 342 | 7 | Wood Handle Griddle | |
| 343 | 8 | Wood Handle Griddle | |
| 344 | 4 | Utility Bowl with wood handles – aluminum | |
| 345 | 5 | Utility Bowl with wood handles – aluminum | |
| 347 | 2 | Mailbox body | |
| 348 | | Mailbox lid for p/n 347 | |
| 350 | | Mailbox hinge block | |
| 352 | 50 | Food Chopper screw | |
| 353 | | Mailbox top | see p/n 361 |
| 354 | 4 | Mailbox body | see p/n 355 & 356 |
| 355 | | Mailbox top | |
| 356 | | Mailbox top door | |
| 357 | | Sundial; also Mailbox, very early, no No. | |
| 358 | | Mailbox top flap for p/n 357 | |
| 361 | | Mailbox top door | see p/n 353 |
| 363 | 11 | Square Waffle Iron (male ball joint) | frame p/n 986 or 987 |
| 364 | 11 | Square Waffle Iron (female ball joint) | frame p/n 986 or 987 |
| 366 | | Waffle Iron, rectangular, 3-section, patent 1908 | frame No. 12, 13 or 14 |
| 367 | | Waffle Iron, rectangular, 3-section, patent 1908 | frame No. 12, 13 or 14 |
| 371 | 10 | Wood Handled Skillet | |
| 372 | 11 | Wood Handled Skillet | |
| 373 | 12 | Wood Handled Skillet | |
| 380 | 1 | Mailbox body | late style |
| 381 | | Mailbox door | for p/n 380 |
| 382 | | Mailbox lid or top | for p/n 380 |
| 385 | 2 | Tobacco Cutter base | |
| 386 | 2 | Tobacco Cutter upper body half, back | |
| 387 | 2 | Tobacco Cutter upper body half, front | |

| P/N | NO. | ITEM | Other Information |
|-----|-----|------|-------------------|
| 388 | 2 | Tobacco Cutter handle | |
| 389 | 2 | Tobacco Cutter blade clasp | |
| 390 | 2 | Tobacco Cutter blade pivot | |
| 391 | 2 | Tobacco Cutter base | |
| 394 | | Tobacco Cutter blade clasp | |
| 395 | 8 | Waffle Iron, marked VICTOR or GOOD HEALTH | 1922 patent or later |
| 396 | | Waffle frame, low, side handle, no drip ring | for Victor irons |
| 397 | | Tobacco Cutter handle | |
| 398 | 8 | Waffle frame, low, bailed handle | for irons p/n 395 |
| 401 | 0 | Food Chopper body | |
| 402 | 0 | Food Chopper scroll | |
| 403 | 0 | Food Chopper crank | |
| 404 | 0 | Food Chopper nut butter knife | |
| 406 | 0 | Toy Waffle Iron (male ball joint) | |
| 407 | 0 | Toy Waffle Iron (female ball joint) | |
| 408 | 0 | Toy Waffle Iron frame, low, side handle | |
| 409 | 50 | Food Chopper body | |
| 410 | 50 | Food Chopper scroll | |
| 411 | 1 | Skillet | (same size as No. 0 skillet) |
| 432 | 0,1,2,3,4 | Wing Nut for Food Chopper | |
| 434 | 50 | Food Chopper handle | |
| 450 | 1 | Food Chopper body | |
| 451 | 1 | Food Chopper ring | |
| 453 | 2 | Food Chopper body | |
| 454 | 2 & 3 | Food Chopper ring | |
| 456 | 3 | Food Chopper body | |
| 458 | 4 | Food Chopper body | |
| 459 | 4 | Food Chopper ring | |
| 463 | 3 | Self Basting Skillet Cover, low | |
| 465 | 5 | Self Basting Skillet Cover, low | |
| 466 | 6 | Self Basting Skillet Cover, low | |
| 467 | 7 | Self Basting Skillet Cover, low | |
| 468 | 8 | Self Basting Skillet Cover, low | |
| 469 | 9 | Self Basting Skillet Cover, low | |
| 470 | 10 | Self Basting Skillet Cover, low | |
| 471 | 11 | Self Basting Skillet Cover, low | |
| 472 | 12 | Self Basting Skillet Cover, low | |
| 474 | 14 | Self Basting Skillet Cover, low | |
| 479 | 9 | PURITAN Dutch Oven (made for Sears) | see p/n 189, 1521 |
| 482 | 9 | Cover for Dutch Oven, unmarked | see p/n *479 |
| 491 | 9 | Dutch Oven, not marked | see p/n 494 |
| 494 | 9 | Dutch Oven Cover, not marked | see p/n 491 |
| 500 | 3" | Damper | see p/n 1423 |
| 506 | 6 | Griddle | |
| 508 | 5" | Damper | |
| 510 | 3" | Oval Damper | |
| 511 | 5 1/2" | Damper | |
| 512 | | 2 qt. Tea Kettle | |
| 517 | 6" | Round Damper, early | |
| 520 | 6" | Damper | |
| 522 | 3" | Damper | |
| 523 | 4" | Damper | |
| 532 | | 2 qt. Tea Kettle | |
| 538 | 6" | Damper | |
| 541 | 4" | Oval Damper | |
| 562 | 0 | Toy Skillet | |
| 565 | 0 | Toy Regular Griddle | |
| 568 | 0 | Toy Tite-Top Dutch Oven | |
| 569 | 0 | Cover for Toy Tite-Top Dutch Oven | see p/n 568 |
| 570 | 00 | Ashtray Skillet with matchbook holder | |
| 573 | 00 | Trivet for Toy Tite-Top Dutch Oven | see p/n 568 |
| 575 | 000 | Service Kettle | |

| P/N | NO. | ITEM | Other Information |
|-----|-----|------|-------------------|
| 576 | 0 | Colonial Design Toy Tea Kettle | 1 1/4 pts. capacity |
| 578 | 000 | Serving Kettle, 3-legs, short | cover is p/n 581 |
| 579 | 00 | Serving Kettle, 3-legs, long | cover is p/n 581 |
| 580 | 0 | Service Kettle | |
| 581 | 0 | Cover for p/n 109, 578, 579 & 580 | |
| 603 | 3 PT | Casserole | |
| 606 | 6 | Regular Griddle | later than p/n 736 |
| 607 | 7 | Regular Griddle | later than p/n 737 |
| 608 | 8 | Regular Griddle | later than p/n 738 |
| 609 | 9 | Regular Griddle | later than p/n 739 |
| 610 | 10 | Regular Griddle | later than p/n 740 |
| 611 | 6 | Wood Handle Griddle | |
| 613 | 8 | Wood Handle Griddle | |
| 615 | 10 | Wood Handle Griddle | |
| 616 | 10 | Bailed Griddle | later than p/n 776 |
| 617 | 12 | Bailed Griddle | later than p/n 741 |
| 618 | 14 | Bailed Griddle | later than p/n 742 |
| 619 | 16 | Bailed Griddle | |
| 620 | 8 | Good Health Handle Griddle | |
| 625 | 262 | Corn or Wheat Stick Pan | tiny size, corn pattern |
| 629 | 272 | Corn or Wheat Stick Pan | corn or wheat pattern, 7 sticks |
| 630 | 282 | Corn or Wheat Stick Pan | like p/n 629 but larger |
| 631 | 240 | Turk Head Muffin Pan | 12 cups |
| 632 | 2700 | Wheat & Corn Stick Pan | wheat pattern, 7 sticks |
| 633 | 2800 | Wheat & Corn Stick Pan | like p/n 632 but larger |
| 634 | 130 | Turk Head Muffin Pan | like p/n 635 but 6 cups |
| 635 | 140 | Turk Head Muffin Pan | 12 cups |
| 636 | 270 | Corn or Wheat Stick Pan | like p/n 629 but ears alternate |
| 637 | 280 | Corn or Wheat Stick Pan | like p/n 636 but larger |
| 638 | 27 | Wheat & Corn Stick Pan or Whole Wheat Stick Pan | wheat pattern, 6 sticks |
| 639 | 28 | Wheat & Corn Stick Pan or Whole Wheat Stick Pan | like p/n 638 but larger |
| 640 | 13 | Turk Head Muffin Pan | 6 cups, cutouts |
| 641 | 14 | Turk Head Muffin Pan | 12 cups, cutouts; see p/n 952 |
| 643 | 3 | Oval Roaster | see p/n 2627 for earlier style |
| 644 | 3 | Oval Roaster Cover | see p/n 2628 |
| 645 | 5 | Oval Roaster | see p/n 2629 for earlier style |
| 646 | 5 | Oval Roaster Cover | see p/n 2630 |
| 647 | 7 | Oval Roaster | see p/n 2631 for earlier style |
| 648 | 7 | Oval Roaster Cover | see p/n 2632 |
| 649 | 9 | Oval Roaster | |
| 650 | 9 | Oval Roaster Cover | |
| 653 | 3 | Good Health Skillet, not marked Griswold | |
| 656 | 6 | Good Health Skillet, not marked Griswold | |
| 658 | 8 | Good Health Skillet, not marked Griswold | |
| 659 | 9 | Good Health Skillet, not marked Griswold | |
| 664 | 14 | Good Health Skillet, not marked Griswold | |
| 665 | | Breakfast Skillet, large, round, 5-sections | |
| 666 | | Colonial Breakfast Skillet | |
| 667 | 8 | "50th Anniversary No.8 (skillet) King HDW. CO." | not marked Griswold |
| 668 | 3 | Skillet, not marked, 3 holes in handle | |
| 669 | 4 | Skillet, not marked, 3 holes in handle | |
| 674 | | Drilled Burner for stove series 704, 720, 734, 820 & 8020 | |
| 677 | | Drilled Giant Burner (used with p/n 681) will fit series 700 & 800 | |
| 681 | | Simmering Burner (used with p/n 677) will fit series 700 & 800 | |
| 683 | | Stove Burner used on stoves Nos. 150-160 | |
| 689 | | Star Burner for stoves 700, 710, 730, 800, 7032, 7033, 7120, 7232, 7130, 7233 | |
| 690 | | Star Giant Burner for stoves 700, 710, 730, 800, 7032, 7033, 7120, 7232, 7130, 7233 | |
| 694 | 14 | Skillet, bail handle, pouring lip opposite handle | |
| 695 | 5 | Victor Skillet | |
| 697 | 6 | Victor Skillet | |
| 698 | 6 | Wood Handled Skillet | |
| 699B | 6 | Skillet with smoke ring | |

| P/N | NO. | ITEM | Other Information |
|---|---|---|---|
| 700 | 5 | Wood Handled Skillet | |
| 701 | 7 | Skillet | |
| 701A | 7 | Skillet | |
| 701F | 7 | Skillet | |
| 702 | 4 | Skillet | |
| 703 | 2 | Skillet | |
| 704 | 8 | Skillet | |
| 704D | 8 | Skillet | |
| 705 | 8 | N.E. Griddle | |
| 706 | 9 | N.E. Griddle | |
| 707 | 10 | N.E. Griddle | |
| 709 | 3 | Skillet | |
| 710 | 9 | Skillet | |
| 711 | 7 | Oval Griddle | |
| 712 | 8 | Oval Griddle | |
| 713 | 9 | Oval Griddle | |
| 715 | 8 | Skillet w/ extra thick, smooth, unmarked bottom; Griswold and 715 under handle | |
| 716 | 10 | Skillet | |
| 717 | 11 | Skillet | |
| 718 | 14 | Skillet | |
| 719 | 12 | Skillet | |
| 719B | 12 | Skillet | |
| 720 | 13 | Skillet | |
| 721 | 7 | Victor Skillet | see p/n 695 & 697 |
| 722 | 8 | Victor Skillet | |
| 723 | 9 | Victor Skillet | |
| 724 | 5 | Skillet | |
| 725 | 7 | Wood Handled Skillet | |
| 726 | 8 | Wood Handled Skillet | |
| 727 | 9 | Wood Handled Skillet | |
| 728 | 20 | Skillet with smoke ring | Two loop handles |
| 729 | 8A | Shallow Skillet 3 holes in handle | |
| 730 | 9 | Shallow Skillet | |
| 731 | 10A | Skillet Griddle | |
| 732 | 8 | Deep Skillet (this one is older than 777 & wider at the top) | |
| 733 | 9 | Deep Skillet | |
| 734 | 10 | Deep Skillet | |
| 735 | 2 | Wood Handled Skillet | |
| 736 | 6 | Regular Griddle | earlier than p/n 606 |
| 737 | 7 | Regular Griddle | earlier than p/n 607 |
| 738 | 8 | Regular Griddle | earlier than p/n 608 |
| 739 | 9 | Regular Griddle | earlier than p/n 609 |
| 740 | 10 | Regular Griddle | earlier than p/n 610 |
| 741 | 12 | Bailed Griddle | earlier than p/n 617 |
| 742 | 14 | Bailed Griddle | earlier than p/n 618 |
| 743 | 16 | Bailed Griddle | early |
| 744 | 7 | Long Griddle | |
| 745 | 8 | Long Griddle | |
| 746 | 9 | Long Griddle | see p/n *771 |
| 749 | 8 | Long Pan or Iron Heater, deep pattern | see p/n 752 |
| 752 | 8 | Long Pan or Iron Heater, shallow pattern | see p/n 749 |
| 753 | 3 | Wood Handled Skillet | |
| 754 | 7 | Skillet, like Victor, but marked only with pattern number | |
| 755 | 8 | Skillet, like Victor, but marked only with pattern number | |
| 758 | 4 | Wood Handle Skillet | |
| 763 | 4 | Side Handled Griddle, 11 inch, (export ware) | |
| 768 | 8 | Square Fry Skillet or Square Utility Skillet; handle at corner | |
| 769 | 18 | Long Griddle, pat. 11-14-16, trough around perimeter (size 8) | |
| 770 | | Square Ashtray with matchbook holder | |
| 771 | | Folding Griddle, part marked G. MFG. CO., ERIE, PA (end section) | |
| 772 | | Folding Griddle, part marked PAT'D FEB. 6TH 1883 (end section) | |

| P/N | NO. | ITEM | Other Information |
|---|---|---|---|
| 773 | | Folding Griddle, part marked only with pattern No. (center section) | |
| 774 | 12 | Erie Gas Griddle, bottom part | see p/n 847 |
| 775 | | Square Toy Skillet | |
| 776 | 10 | Bailed Griddle | earlier than p/n 616 |
| 777 | 8 | Extra Deep Skillet, marked Cast Iron Skillet or Chicken Pan (Not on all pans) | |
| 778 | 9 | Extra Deep Skillet | |
| 779 | 10 | Extra Deep Skillet | |
| 780 | 2 | Scotch Bowl | |
| 781 | 3 | Scotch Bowl | |
| 782 | 4 | Scotch Bowl | |
| 783 | 5 | Scotch Bowl | |
| 784 | 2 | Yankee Bowl | |
| 785 | 3 | Yankee Bowl | |
| 786 | 4 | Yankee Bowl | |
| 788 | 6 | Regular Kettle | 3-leg |
| 789 | 7 | Regular Kettle | 3-leg |
| 791 | 8 | Regular Kettle | |
| 792 | 9 | Regular Kettle | |
| 794 | 7 | Regular Bulged Pot | 3-leg |
| 795 | 8 | Regular Bulged Pot (3-let) | 3-leg |
| 796 | 9 | Regular Bulged Pot | 3-leg |
| 797 | 7 | Low Kettle | 3-leg |
| 803 | 7 | Rimmed Pot | 3-leg |
| 809 | 6 | Flat Bottom Kettle | cover is p/n 867 |
| 810 | 7 | Flat Bottom Kettle | cover is p/n 868 |
| 811 | 8 | Flat Bottom Kettle | cover is p/n 881 |
| 812 | 9 | Flat Bottom Kettle | |
| 813 | 7 | Flat Bottom Bulged Pot | |
| 814 | 8 | Flat Bottom Bulged Pot | |
| 815 | | Flat Bottom Bulged Pot | |
| 816 | 7 | Eccentric Kettle | |
| 817 | 8 | Eccentric Kettle | |
| 820 | | Barbecue Grill Coal Tray | |
| 821 | | Barbecue Grill | |
| 824 | 8 | Low Eccentric Kettle | |
| 827 | 8 | Extra Large Eccentric Pot, style "B" | |
| 833 | 8 | Dutch Oven | see p/n 2603 for size 7 |
| 834 | 9 | Dutch Oven | |
| 835 | 10 | Dutch Oven | see p/n 839, 2553 |
| 836 | 11 | Dutch Oven | also with 3 legs, see p/n 2634 |
| 837 | No. 2 | Scotch Bowl with flat bottom | |
| 838 | No. 3 | Scotch Bowl with flat bottom | |
| 839 | 10 | Dutch Oven Cover | fits p/n 835 |
| 840 | 11 | Dutch Oven Cover | fits p/n 836 |
| 841 | 8 | Flanged Dutch Oven Cover | |
| 842 | 9 | Flanged Dutch Oven Cover | |
| 843 | 10 | Flanged Dutch Oven Cover | fits p/n 180, 310 |
| 844 | 11 | Flanged Dutch Oven Cover | |
| 845 | | Table Service Casserole | larger than p/n 853 |
| 846 | 7 | Erie Tea Kettle | pit bottom, see p/n *856, *851 |
| 847 | No. 12 | Bailed Griddle part of Erie Gas Griddle | see p/n 774 |
| 848 | | Steak Platter, 7" x 10" | |
| 849 | | Steak Platter, 7 3/4" x 11 3/4" | |
| 850 | 9 | Hot Service Plate | |
| 851 | | Steak Platter, 8 3/4" x 12" | |
| 853 | | Table Service Casserole | smaller than p/n 845 |
| 854 | | lid for p/n 853 | |
| 855 | 7 1/2 | Hot Service Plate | |
| 856 | | Steak Platter, 9 1/4" x 13 5/8" | |
| 858 | 8 | Safety Cooker, flat bottom (some have TM and Skinner Safety Co.) | |
| 859 | | Loaf Pan Cover for p/n 877 | |
| 860 | 10 | Flat Bottom Kettle | see p/n *883 |
| 861 | 9 | Safety Cooker, three legged round bottom | see p/n 858 |

| P/N | NO. | ITEM | Other Information |
|-----|-----|------|-------------------|
| 862 | | Rabbit Cake Mold (front) | see p/n 1005 |
| 863 | | Rabbit Cake Mold (back) | |
| 865 | | Lamb Cake Mold (earlier, but similar to p/n 921/922) | (not marked Griswold) |
| 866 | | Lamb Cake Mold (earlier, but similar to p/n 921/922) | |
| 867 | 6 | Flat Bottom Kettle Cover | see p/n 809 |
| 868 | 7 | Flat Bottom Kettle Cover | see p/n 881 |
| 869 | | Odorless Skillet | Pat'd Oct. 17, 1893 |
| 870 | | Junior Patty Bowl | very small |
| 871 | | Patty Bowl | |
| 872 | | Hinge part for Wafer Iron p/n 895 | |
| 873 | | Nut Cracker | |
| 875 | | Double Broiler (bottom) | see p/n 878/880 |
| 876 | | Double Broiler (top) | |
| 877 | | Loaf Pan | see p/n 859 |
| 878 | | Erie Double Broiler (bottom) | see p/n 880 |
| 880 | | Erie Double Broiler (top) | see p/n 878 |
| 881 | 8 | Flat Bottom Kettle Cover | see p/n 868 |
| 882 | 9 | Flat Bottom Kettle Cover | |
| 883 | 7 | Waffle Frame, low, side handles | for p/n 888 irons |
| 884 | 8 | Waffle Frame, low, side handle | for p/n 976/977 irons |
| 885 | No. 8 | Waffle Iron (1908 patent and also without) | female ball joint |
| 886 | No. 8 | Waffle Iron (1908 patent and also without) | male ball joint |
| 888 | No. 7 & 8 | Waffle Iron (1880 & 1893 pat., finger & slot joint; frame p/n 883) | |
| 889 | No. 7 | Waffle Iron (1908 patent and somewhat earlier) frame 2428, 972 | |
| 890 | No. 7 | Waffle Iron (as above, the other half; tit at 3 & 9 o'clock) | |
| 894 | | Frame for Wafer Irons p/n 895 and (995)? | |
| 895 | | Wafer Iron Half; other half may be 995 | 1880 patent |
| 897 | | Santa Claus Cake Mold (front) | |
| 898 | | Santa Claus Cake Mold (back) | |
| 900 | No. 2 | Waffle Frame, rectangular | p/n 904/905 irons |
| 901 | No. 1 | Waffle Frame, rectangular | p/n 906/907 irons |
| 902 | No. 0 | Waffle Frame, rectangular | p/n 908/909 irons |
| 903 | No. 00 | Waffle Frame, rectangular | p/n 910/911 irons |
| 904 | No. 2 | Waffle Iron, rectangular, 3 cakes | frame p/n 900 |
| 905 | No. 2 | Waffle Iron, rectangular, 3 cakes | frame p/n 900 |
| 906 | No. 1 | Waffle Iron, rectangular, 3 cakes | frame p/n 901 |
| 907 | No. 1 | Waffle Iron, rectangular, 3 cakes | frame p/n 901 |
| 908 | No. 0 | Waffle Iron, rectangular, 4 cakes | frame p/n 902 |
| 909 | No. 0 | Waffle Iron, rectangular, 4 cakes | frame p/n 902 |
| 910 | No. 00 | Waffle Iron, rectangular, 6 cakes | frame p/n 903 |
| 911 | No. 00 | Waffle Iron, rectangular, 6 cakes | frame p/n 903 |
| 913 | No. 8 | Waffle Frame, low, bailed handle | p/n 314/315, p/n 919/920 |
| 915 | No. 8 | Waffle Frame. high, bailed handle | p/n 314/315, p/n 919/920 |
| 916 | No. 7 | Oval Waffle Frame | p/n *921/922 irons |
| 917 | No. 8 | Oval Waffle Frame | p/n 923/924 irons |
| 918 | | Flat Bottle Kettle with side handles | |
| 919 | No. 18 | Waffle Iron, Heart Star, 1920 pat., size 8 | see p/n 929 |
| 920 | No. 18 | Waffle Iron, Heart Star, 1920 pat., size 9 | see p/n 928 |
| 921 | No. 866 | Lamb Cake Mold (back) | later than p/n 865/866 |
| 922 | No. 866 | Lamb Cake Mold (front) | later than p/n 865/866 |
| 923 | No. 8 | Oval Waffle Iron | frame p/n 917 |
| 924 | No. 8 | Oval Waffle Iron | |
| 925 | No. 9 | Oval Waffle Iron | |
| 926 | No. 9 | Oval Waffle Iron | |
| 928 | No. 18 | Waffle Iron, Heart Star, 1922 pat., size 8 | see p/n 919/920 |
| 929 | No. 19 | Waffle Iron, Heart Star, 1922 pat., size 9 | see p/n 932/933 |
| 930 | No. 273 | Corn Stick Pan | |
| 931 | No. 283 | Corn Stick Pan, large | |
| 932 | No. 19 | Waffle Iron, Heart Star, 1920 pat., size 9 | see p/n 929 |
| 933 | No. 19 | Waffle Iron, Heart Star, 1920 pat., size 9 | see p/n 929 |
| 934 | | French Waffle Iron, with three waffles | |
| 935 | | French Waffle Iron, with three waffles | |

| P/N | NO. | ITEM | Other Information |
|---|---|---|---|
| 936 | 4 qt. | Maslin Kettle | |
| 937 | 6 qt. | Maslin Kettle | |
| 938 | 8 qt. | Maslin Kettle | |
| 939 | 12 qt. | Maslin Kettle | |
| 940 | No. 1 | Muffin Pan, 11 cups | |
| 941 | No. 2 | Muffin Pan, 11 cups | |
| 942 | No. 3 | Muffin Pan, 11 cups | |
| 943 | No. 5 | Muffin Pan, 8 cups | |
| 944 | No. 6 | Muffin Pan, 11 cups | see p/n 958 |
| 945 | No. 7 | Muffin Pan, 8 cups | |
| 946 | No. 8 | Muffin Pan, 8 cups | |
| 947 | No. 9 | Golf Ball Pan or Brownie Cake Pan, 12 cups | see p/n 966 |
| 948 | No. 10 | Popover Pan (top edge follows cup contour) | see p/n 2070 |
| 949 | No. 10 | Popover Pan (top edge is straight), 11 cups | |
| 950 | No.11 | Muffin Pan, 12 cups | |
| 951 | No.12 | Muffin Pan, 11 cups | |
| 952 | No.14 | Erie Muffin Pan, 12 rectangular cups | see p/n 641 |
| 953 | No.20 | Turk head pan, 11 cups | |
| 954 | No.22 | Corn Bread Pan (bread stick pan), 11 sticks | |
| 955 | No.23 | Bread Stick Pan, 22 short sticks | |
| 956 | No. 2 | Vienna Roll Bread Pan, 2 loaves | |
| 957 | No.24 | Corn Bread Pan (identical to 961 but not marked Griswold) | |
| 958 | No.26 | Vienna Bread (roll) Pan (early pans are marked No. 6) | |
| 959 | No.50 | Hearts star gem pan, small; six hearts, six-pointed star | |
| 960 | No.100 | Hearts star gem pan; five hearts, five-pointed star | |
| 961 | No.21 | Corn bread pan (bread stick pan), 7 sticks | |
| 962 | No.32 | Egg poacher or apple cake pan or danish cake pan | |
| 963 | No.31 | Danish cake pan (flat top) | see p/n 962 |
| 964 | | Sealing Wax Ladle, Erie | |
| 965 | | Cake Mold (bundt pan) | |
| 966 | No.19 | Golfball Pan, 6 cups | |
| 967 | No.6 | Waffle iron | see p/n 970/971 |
| 968 | No.7 | Waffle iron | see p/n 972, 973 |
| 969 | | Plett Pan (marked GRI SW OLD on bottom) | |
| 970 | 6 | Waffle Frame, low, side handle | see p/n 967/971 irons |
| 971 | No.6 | Waffle iron | see p/n 967, 970 |
| 972 | 7 | Waffle Frame, low, side handle | p/n 889/890, 968/973 irons |
| 973 | No.7 | Waffle iron | see p/n 968, 972 |
| 975 | 8 | Waffle frame, low, side handle | p/n 885/886; 976/977 irons |
| 976 | No.8 | Waffle iron | |
| 977 | No.8 | Waffle iron | |
| 978 | 9 | Waffle iron, low, side handle | p/n 979/980 irons |
| 979 | No.9 | Waffle iron | Frame p/n 778, 2429 |
| 980 | No.9 | Waffle iron | Frame p/n 778, 2429 |
| 981 | | Alfred Andresen heart shaped design waffle | see p/n 999 |
| 982 | 8 | Victor Waffle Frame, low, for early Victor Irons | p/n 983/984 irons |
| 983 | No.8 | Victor Waffle Iron | frame p/n 982 |
| 984 | No.8 | Victor Waffle Iron | frame p/n 982 |
| 985 | 8 | Waffle Frame, high, side handles | p/n 885/886 irons |
| 986 | No.11 | Square Waffle Frame, low, side handle | p/n 363/364 irons |
| 987 | No.11 | Square Waffle Frame, high, bailed handle | p/n 363/364 irons |
| 988 | No. 11 | Square Waffle Iron, 1901 patent | |
| 989 | No.11 | Square Waffle Iron, 1901 patent | |
| 990 | No.12 | Square Waffle Frame, for two rectangular irons | |
| 991 | No. 13 | Rectangular Waffle Frame, for three rectangular irons | |
| 992 | No. 14 | Rectangular Waffle Frame, for four rectangular irons | |
| 993 | | Waffle Iron, rectangular, 3-section, pat. 1901 | No. 12, 13, 14 frames |
| 994 | | Waffle Iron, rectangular, 3-section, pat. 1901 | No. 12, 13, 14 frames |
| 995 | | Wafer Iron | see p/n 885 |
| 999 | | Alfred Andresen heart shaped design waffle | see p/n 981 |
| 1003 | | Deep Fat Fryer with wire basket | |
| 1008 | 8 | Dinner Skillet, All-In-One | 3 sections, cover 1048 |

| P/N | NO. | ITEM | Other Information |
|---|---|---|---|
| 1012 | No. 13 | Oval Skillet | |
| 1013 | No. 15 | Oval Skillet | cover p/n 1013c |
| 1015 | No. 16 1/2 | Oval Skillet | |
| 1018 | | Skillet Divider insert for No. 8 Skillet | 3 sections |
| 1021 | 90 | Double Skillet Bottom | |
| 1022 | 90 | Double Skillet Top | |
| 1029 | 4 | Skillet, not marked, has heat ring and distinctive handle | |
| 1030 | 5 | Skillet, not marked, has heat ring and distinctive handle | see p/n 1081 |
| 1031 | 3 | Skillet, not marked, has heat ring and distinctive handle | |
| 1032 | 7 | Skillet, not marked, has heat ring and distinctive handle | |
| 1033 | 8 | Skillet, not marked, has heat ring and distinctive handle | |
| 1034 | 8 | Deep Skillet or Chicken Fryer, as above | uses cover p/n 1035 |
| 1035 | 8 | Skillet Cover, high, not marked | used on p/n 1034 |
| 1036 | 8 | Dutch Oven, not marked | uses cover p/n 1037 |
| 1037 | 8 | Cover for Dutch Oven above, not marked | |
| 1038 | 9 | Dutch Oven, not marked | uses cover p/n 1039 |
| 1039 | 9 | Cover for Dutch Oven above, not marked | |
| 1040 | 10 | Dutch Oven, not marked | uses cover p/n 1041 |
| 1041 | 10 | Cover for Dutch Oven above, not marked | |
| 1047 | 7 | Self Basting Skillet Cover, high | |
| 1048 | 8 | Self Basting Skillet Cover, high | |
| 1049 | 9 | Self Basting Skillet Cover, high | |
| 1050 | 10 | Self Basting Skillet Cover, high | |
| 1056 | 8 inch | Steak Plate | |
| 1064 | | "Griswold" casting used on front of Skillet and Griddle Display Racks | |
| 1065 | | Dutch Oven Display Stand, top castings | |
| 1069 | | 5-Tier Dutch Oven Display Rack, top TM Casting | |
| 1078 | 8 | Long Griddle, not marked Griswold | |
| 1081 | 6 | Skillet, not marked, has heat ring and distinctive handle | see p/n 1030 |
| 1082 | 9 | Skillet, not marked, has heat ring and distinctive handle | |
| 1083 | 10 | Skillet, not marked, has heat ring and distinctive handle | |
| 1085 | 14 | Skillet, not marked, has heat ring and distinctive handle | |
| 1088 | 8 | Skillet Cover, low, not marked | fits p/n 1033 |
| 1093 | 3 | Skillet Lid, high, smooth top (some of this series will have a raised trademark on top of the lid) | |
| 1094 | 4 | Skillet Lid, high, smooth top " | |
| 1095 | 5 | Skillet Lid, high, smooth top " | |
| 1096 | 6 | Skillet Lid, high, smooth top | |
| 1097 | 7 | Skillet Lid, high, smooth top | |
| 1098 | 8 | Skillet Lid, high, smooth top | |
| 1099 | 9 | Skillet Lid, high, smooth top | see p/n 1000 for size 10 |
| 1100 | 10 | Skillet Lid, high, smooth top | |
| 1102 | 80 | Double Skillet Bottom | size 8 |
| 1103 | 80 | Double Skillet Top | size 8 |
| 1108 | No. 18 | Cast Iron Grill | |
| 1124 | No. 2020 | Elevated Gas Hot Plate, 2 burner | |
| 1131 | No. 31 | Gas Hot Plate, 1 burner | |
| 1160 | | Star Burner for Gas Hot Plate; series nos. 400, 500, 600, 4200, 4030 | |
| 1161 | | Drilled Burner for Gas Hot Plate; will fit same series as above | |
| 1168 | No. 401 | Gas Hot Plate, 1 burner | |
| 1169 | No. 402 | Gas Hot Plate, 2 burners | |
| 1171 | No. 32 | Gas Hot Plate, 2 burners | |
| 1172 | | Legs for Gas Hot Plate No. 502 | |
| 1173 | | Legs for Gas Hot Plate No. 501, 502 | |
| 1178 | No. 501 | Gas Hot Plate, 1 burner | |
| 1180 | | Loose Cap Burner for Gas Hot Plate; | fit series No. 500 |
| 1181 | No. 502 | Gas Hot Plate, 2 burners | see p/n 1173 |
| 1182 | No. 503 | Gas Hot Plate, 3 burners | see p/n 1183 |
| 1183 | | Legs for Gas Hot Plate No. 503, wishbone style | |
| 1206 | | Skillet with cover and wood handle – aluminum | |
| 1208 | | Skillet with cover and wood handle – aluminum | |
| 1233 | No. 3 | Best Made S.R. and Co., Skillet (made for Sears) | |
| 1235 | No. 5 | Best Made S.R. and Co., Skillet (made for Sears) | |

| P/N | NO. | ITEM | Other Information |
|---|---|---|---|
| 1236 | No. 6 | Best Made S.R. and Co., Skillet (made for Sears) | |
| 1238 | No. 8 | Best Made S.R. and Co., Skillet (made for Sears) | |
| 1239 | No. 9 | Best Made S.R. and Co., Skillet (made for Sears) | |
| 1240 | No. 10 | Best Made S.R. and Co., Skillet (made for Sears) | |
| 1243 | No. 9 | Best Made S.R. and Co., self basting skillet cover, low | |
| 1250 | | Best Made S.R. and Co., Waffle Irons | frame p/n 1251 |
| 1251 | | Best Made S.R. and Co., Waffle Frame, low, side handle, irons p/n 1250 | |
| 1253 | No. 10 | Best Made S.R. and Co., Popover Pan | like p/n 948 |
| 1257 | | Best Made Bacon and Egg Fryer (made for Sears) | almost like p/n 666 |
| 1258 | No. 8 | Best Made S.R. and Co., Dutch Oven (made for Sears) | cover is p/n 1261 |
| 1259 | No. 9 | Best Made S.R. and Co., Dutch Oven (made for Sears) | cover is p/n 1262 |
| 1261 | No. 8 | Best Made S.R. and Co., Dutch Oven Cover | for p/n 1258 |
| 1262 | No. 9 | Best Made S.R. and Co., Dutch Oven Cover | for p/n 1259 |
| 1265 | No. 9 | Trivet | for p/n 1259 |
| 1270 | No. 1270 | S.R. and Co., Best Made Wheat & Corn Stick Pan | like p/n 632; see p/n 1513 |
| 1277 | 7 | Tite-Top Dutch Oven | 1930's and later |
| 1278 | 8 | Tite-Top Dutch Oven | 1930's and later |
| 1279 | 9 | Tite-Top Dutch Oven | 1930's and later |
| 1288 | 8 | Cover for Dutch Oven | p/n 1278 |
| 1289 | 9 | Cover for Dutch Oven | p/n 1279 |
| 1295 | 8 | Tite-Top Dutch Oven, no bail, small round hole in handles | |
| 1298 | 8 | Deep Tite-Top Dutch Oven | same style as p/n 1278 |
| 1308 | size 3 | Sad iron, top plate casting | |
| 1313 | | Classic Sad Iron Heater, round pattern | p/n 2485 is sq. pattern |
| 1332 | | Loose Cap Burner for Gas Hot Plate; will fit series No. 1000 | |
| 1335 | | Food Chopper Stand | |
| 1423 | 3" | Damper | see p/n 500 |
| 1424 | 4" | Damper | |
| 1425 | 5" | Damper | |
| 1426 | 6" | Damper | |
| 1428 | 8" | Damper | |
| 1457 | | Stove Burner used in Stoves Nos. 130-140 | |
| 1462 | | Stove Burner used in Stoves Nos. 230-250-260-270 | |
| 1482 | | Lard Pot or grease pot, square w/bail and pouring lip | |
| 1501 | 3 | Merit Skillet (made for Sears), has distinctive handle | |
| 1502 | 5 | Merit Skillet (made for Sears), has distinctive handle | |
| 1503 | 7 | Merit Skillet (made for Sears), has distinctive handle | |
| 1504 | 8 | Puritan Skillet (made for Sears), has distinctive handle | |
| 1507 | 8 | Puritan Handled Griddle (made for Sears) | |
| 1508 | 9 | Handled Griddle marked Merit | |
| 1512 | No. 10 | Puritan Popover Pan (made for Sears) | similar to p/n 848 |
| 1513 | No. 1270 | Puritan or Merit Wheat Stick Pan (Sears) | different than p/n 1270 |
| 1521 | 9 | Puritan Dutch Oven Cover (made for Sears) | see p/n 479 |
| 1522 | 10 | Merit Dutch Oven Cover (made for Sears) | |
| 1528 | | Rarebit Dish | |
| 1529 | | Rarebit Dish | |
| 1556 | No. 2 | Charcoal Furnace | |
| 1602 | | Classic Sad Iron Trivet | |
| 1618 | | Removable grate for Gas Hot Plate No. 703 | see p/n 1679 |
| 1679 | No. 703 | Gas Hot Plate, 3 burners | see p/n 674, 1618, 2547 |
| 1688 | | Leg for Gas Hot Plate | |
| 1691 | | Drilled Giant Double Burner; fits series No. 700, 800 gas hot plates | |
| 1701 | | Leg for Gas Hot Plate; used on most of the common hot plates | |
| 1707 | | Clamp screw and button for food chopper Nos. 1, 2, 3, 4 | |
| 1708 | | Wing Nut for Food Chopper Nos. 1, 2, 3, 4 | |
| 1711 | | Body for Food Chopper No. 1 | |
| 1712 | | Body for Food Chopper No. 2 | |
| 1713 | | Body for Food Chopper No. 3 | |
| 1714 | | Body for Food Chopper No. 4 | |
| 1721 | | Ring for Food Chopper No. 1 | |
| 1722 | | Ring for Food Chopper Nos. 2, 3 | |
| 1724 | | Ring for Food Chopper No. 4 | |

| P/N | NO. | ITEM | Other Information |
|---|---|---|---|
| 1725 | | Decorative Flat Iron Trivet, large | see p/n 1900 |
| 1726 | | Decorative Tree Trivet, large | see p/n 1901 |
| 1727 | | Decorative Hex Trivet, large | see p/n 1902 |
| 1728 | | Decorative Broom and Wheat Trivet, large | see p/n 1903 |
| 1729 | | Decorative Floral Trivet, large | see p/n 1904 |
| 1730 | | Decorative Wreath and Eagle Trivet, large | see p/n 1905 |
| 1731 | | Scroll for Food Chopper No. 1 | |
| 1732 | | Scroll for Food Chopper No. 2, 3 | |
| 1733 | | Decorative Flat Iron Trivet, small | see p/n 1906 |
| 1734 | | Scroll for Food Chopper No. 4 | |
| 1735 | | Decorative Tree Trivet, small | see p/n 1907 |
| 1736 | | Decorative Wreath and Eagle Trivet, small | see p/n 1908 |
| 1737 | | Decorative Floral Trivet, small | see p/n 1909 |
| 1738 | | Coffee Pot Trivet, small | |
| 1739 | | Coffee Pot Trivet, large | |
| 1740 | | Star Trivet | |
| 1741 | | Crank for Food Chopper No. 1 | |
| 1742 | | Crank for Food Chopper No. 2, 3 | |
| 1744 | | Crank for Food Chopper No. 4 | |
| 1832 | No. 203 | Gas Hot Plate, 2 burners | see p/n 1834, 1837 |
| 1834 | | Legs for Gas Hot Plate, Nos. 201, 202, 203 | see p/n 185, 187, 1832 |
| 1837 | | Burner for Gas Hot Plate No. 202 | see p/n 1832 |
| 1900 | | Decorative Flat Iron Trivet, large | see p/n 1725 |
| 1901 | | Decorative Tree Trivet, large | see p/n 1726 |
| 1902 | | Decorative Hex Trivet, large | see p/n 1727 |
| 1903 | | Decorative Broom and Wheat Trivet, large | see p/n 1728 |
| 1904 | | Decorative Floral Trivet, large | see p/n 1729 |
| 1905 | | Decorative Wreath and Eagle Trivet, large | see p/n 1730 |
| 1906 | | Decorative Flat Iron Trivet, small | see p/n 1733 |
| 1907 | | Decorative Tree Trivet, small | see p/n 1735 |
| 1908 | | Decorative Wreath and Eagle Trivet, small | see p/n 1736 |
| 1909 | | Decorative Floral Trivet, small | see p/n 1737 |
| 1916 | | Burner for Gas Hot Plate No. 502 | |
| 2003 | 3 | Hammered Skillet | |
| 2005 | 5 | Hammered Skillet | |
| 2008 | 8 | Hammered, Hinge Skillet | cover p/n 2098 |
| 2013 | 3 | Hammered, Hinge Skillet | cover p/n 2093 |
| 2015 | 5 | Hammered, Hinge Skillet | cover p/n 2095 |
| 2028 | 8 | Hammered, Hinge Chicken Fryer | cover p/n 2098 |
| 2039 | 9 | Hammered Handle Griddle | |
| 2040 | 8 | Hammered, Hinge Double Skillet (top) | fits p/n 2028 |
| 2058 | 8 | Hammered, Hinge Dutch Oven | cover p/n 2098 |
| 2070 | No. 10 | Hammered Popover pan | similar to 948 |
| 2073 | No. 273 | Hammered Crispy Corn Stick Pan | similar to 930 |
| 2093 | 3 | Hammered Self-Basting Hinge Skillet Cover | fits p/n 2013 |
| 2095 | 5 | Hammered Self-Basting Hinge Skillet Cover | fits p/n 2015 |
| 2098 | 8 | Hammered Self-Basting Hinge Skillet Cover | fits p/n 2008, 2028, 2058 |
| 2103 | 3 | Square-Fry Skillet | handle at side |
| 2106 | 6 | Square-Fry Skillet | handle at side |
| 2108 | 8 | Square-Fry Skillet | handle at side |
| 2148 | No. 11 | Square Waffle Iron (with or without TM) | frame p/n 987 |
| 2149 | No. 11 | Square Waffle Iron (with or without TM) | frame p/n 987 |
| 2165 | 8 | Dutch Oven - hammered aluminum | |
| 2185 | 5 | Oval Roaster | |
| 2298 | | Scroll for Food Chopper Nos. 2, 3 | |
| 2298 | | Scroll for Food Chopper Nos. 2, 3 | |
| 2301 | | Scroll for Food Chopper No. 1 | |
| 2306 | | Scroll for Food Chopper No. 4 | |
| 2352 | | Clamp Screw and Button for Food Chopper Nos. 0, 1, 2, 3 | |
| 2358 | | Crank for Food Chopper No. 1 | |
| 2361 | | Clamp Screw and Button for Food Chopper No. 4 | |
| 2363 | No. 8 | Ham Boiler | flat bottom |

| P/N | NO. | ITEM | Other Information |
|---|---|---|---|
| 2367 | | Thumb Nut for Food Chopper No. 0 | |
| 2383 | No. 8 | Ham Boiler | |
| 2400 | | Folding pancake griddle, 3 cakes; both sides are solid and identical | |
| 2402 | No. 21 | Waffle Iron, American French Pattern | frame p/n 2404 |
| 2403 | No. 21 | Waffle Iron, American French Pattern | frame p/n 2404 |
| 2404 | No. 21 | American French p/n 21 Waffle, Frame | p/n 2402, 2403 irons |
| 2405 | | Folding Pancake Griddle, 2 cakes, this is the solid side | see p/n 2408 |
| 2406 | | Folding Pancake Griddle, 3 cakes, this is the solid side | see p/n 2408 |
| 2408 | | Folding Pancake Griddle, separate pans for other side of p/n 2405, 2406 | |
| 2428 | No. 77 | Waffle Frame, high, side handles | p/n 889, 890 irons |
| 2429 | No. 9 | Waffle Frame, high, side handles | p/n 979, 980 irons |
| 2434 | 11 | Long Griddle | |
| 2458 | | Food Chopper Crank | for p/n 2460, 450 |
| 2459 | | Food Chopper Scroll | for p/n 2460 |
| 2460 | No. 10 | Food Chopper Body | see p/n 2458, 2459 |
| 2462 | | Top Casting for 6 lb. Sad Iron, large print | |
| 2463 | | Top Casting for 4 lb. Sad Iron, large print | |
| 2469 | | Scroll for Puritan Food Chopper No. 11 | see p/n 2488 |
| 2470 | | Crank for Food Chopper Nos. 2, 3 Puritan No. 11 | see p/n 453, 456, 2488 |
| 2474 | | Crank for Food Chopper No. 4 | see p/n 458 |
| 2485 | | Square Sad Iron Heater | see p/n 1313 |
| 2488 | No. 11 | Body for Puritan Food Chopper | made for Sears |
| 2494 | | Tobacco Cutter Base | |
| 2497 | | Tobacco Cutter Blade Clasp | |
| 2498 | | Tobacco Cutter Lever Arm | |
| 2500 | | Tobacco Cutter Handle | |
| 2503 | 3 | Hinge Skillet | cover p/n 2593 |
| 2505 | 5 | Hinge Skillet | cover p/n 2595 |
| 2506 | 6 | Hinge Skillet | |
| 2507 | 7 | Hinge Skillet | |
| 2508 | 8 | Hinge Skillet | cover p/n 2598 |
| 2509 | 9 | Hinge Skillet | |
| 2528 | 8 | Hinge Chicken Fryer (deep skillet) | cover p/n 2598 |
| 2547 | | Wishbone Leg for Gas Hot Plate No. 703 | see p/n 1679 |
| 2551 | 8 | Cover for Dutch Oven | see p/n 833, 2604 |
| 2552 | 9 | Cover for Dutch Oven | see p/n 834 |
| 2553 | 10 | Cover for Dutch Oven | see p/n 835 |
| 2554 | 11 | Cover for Dutch Oven | see p/n 836, 2636 |
| 2568 | 8 | Hinge Dutch Oven | cover p/n 2598 |
| 2593 | 3 | Self-Basting Hinge Skillet Cover | fits p/n 2503 |
| 2595 | 5 | Self-Basting Hinge Skillet Cover | fits p/n 2505 |
| 2598 | 8 | Self-Basting Hinge Skillet Cover | ftis p/n 2508, 2528, 2568 |
| 2603 | 7 | Dutch Oven | see p/n 833 for size 8 |
| 2604 | 7 | Dutch Oven Cover | see p/n 2551 for size 8 |
| 2605 | 6 | Dutch Oven | |
| 2606 | 6 | Dutch Oven Cover | |
| 2608 | 12 | Waffle Iron with wood handle | |
| 2611 | 2 | Fruit & Lard press & cross bar | |
| 2627 | 3 | Oval Roaster | see p/n 643 for later style |
| 2628 | 3 | Oval Roaster Cover | |
| 2629 | 5 | Oval Roaster | see p/n 645 for later style |
| 2630 | 5 | Oval Roaster Cover | |
| 2631 | 7 | Oval Roaster | see p/n 647 for later style |
| 2632 | 7 | Oval Roaster Cover | |
| 2634 | 12 | Dutch Oven | see p/n 2636, 836 for size 11 |
| 2635 | 13 | Dutch Oven | see p/n 2637 |
| 2636 | 12 | Dutch Oven Cover | see p/n 2634 and 2554 |
| 2637 | 13 | Dutch Oven Cover | see p/n 2635 |
| 2703 | 3 | Skillet, chefs type with bakelite handle, 1950's | |
| 2705 | 5 | Skillet, chefs type with bakelite handle, 1950's | |
| 2708 | 8 | Skillet, chefs type with bakelite handle, 1950's | |
| 2980 | No. 34 | Plett Pan | see p/n 969 |
| 2992 | No. 33 | Munk Pan | |

| P/N | NO. | ITEM | Other Information |
|---|---|---|---|
| 3269 | No. 11 | Square Waffle Iron (male ball joint) | same as p/n 363 |
| 3270 | No. 11 | Square Waffle Iron (female ball joint) | same as p/n 364 |
| 6138 | No. 15 | Muffin Pan, 12 cups | large version of p/n 950 |
| 6139 | No. 16 | Muffin Pan, 6 cups | large version of p/n 6140 |
| 6140 | No. 17 | Muffin Pan, 6 cups | smaller than p/n 6139 |
| 6141 | No. 18 | Popover Pan, 6 cups | |
| 6669 | No. 603 | Gas Hot Plate, 3 burners | see p/n 1160, 1701 |
| 6806 | 5 | Tea Kettle | |
| A16 | | Coffee Pot with base separator | |
| A51 | | Tea Kettle – aluminum | |
| A54L | | Omlet Pan | |
| A54R | | Omlet Pan | |
| A65 | | Bundt Pan – aluminum | |
| A105 | | Coffee Pot with base separator | |
| A128 | | Deep skillet – aluminum | |
| A134 | | 4 pt. Perculator | |
| A152 1/2 | | 2 1/2 qt. Casserole dish and cover | |
| A184 | | 4 pt. Casserole dish | |
| A208C | 8 | Skillet Cover – aluminum | |
| A308 | 8 | Griddle with wood handle – aluminum | |
| A327 | 7 | Rectangular Griddle – aluminum | |
| A412 | 426 | 6 qt. Pot with cover | cover A412C |
| A483 | 3 | Dutch Oven – aluminum | |
| A485 | 5 | Dutch Oven – hammered aluminum | |
| A487 | 7 | Oval Roasters – aluminum | |
| A489 | 9 | Oval Roasters – aluminum | |
| AA-516 | | 2 qt. Tea Kettle | |
| A702 | | 2 qt. Double Broiler with cover and both pans | |
| 710A | 9 | Skillet with smoke ring | |
| 724A | 5 | Skillet – aluminum w/smoke ring | |
| A1208C | | Deep skillet cover – aluminum | |
| A1309 | 9 | Griddle with square wood handle – aluminum | |
| A1485 | 5 | Oval Roaster with cover – aluminum | |
| A1511 | | Saucepan with square handle – aluminum | |
| A1512 | | Saucepan with square handle – aluminum | |
| A1513 | | Saucepan with square handle – aluminum | |
| A2082 | | Meat or Venison Platter with wooden holder | |
| A2135 | | 5 qt. Tea Kettle | |
| A2143 | | 3 qt. Saucepan – hammered aluminum | cover 2143C |
| A2191 | | Family Tree Platter | |
| 2553A | 10 | Tite Top Dutch Oven | |
| A-8011 | 11 | French Roll Pan – cast aluminum | |
| A8018 | 8018 | Popover Pan – aluminum | |
| A8262 | | Tea size cornstick pan | |
| A8273 | 273 | Cornstick Pan – aluminum | |

* – **Duplication of Griswold Pattern Numbers**
p/n – **Pattern Number**
TM – **Trademark**
c. – **Circa Date**

# DUPLICATION OF GRISWOLD PATTERN NUMBERS

The following pattern numbers appeared on two or more different Griswold pieces. This duplication likely happened when a piece was discontinued by Griswold, leaving the pattner number free to use on a new and different piece. This is not a complete list, but only those duplicate pattern numbers that I have seen. Duplicate pattern numbers are marked with an asterisk on the main listing. Compiled by Steve Stephens.

| P/N | NO. | ITEM | Other Information |
|-----|-----|------|-------------------|
| 41 | | 1 pt. Nursery Saucepan with alcohol lamp | |
| 172 | | Water Pitcher - aluminum | |
| 310 | 10 | Dutch Oven, bailed with legs | newer than p/n 180 |
| 314 | 8 | Cake or Omelet Baker Iron | same as waffle iron but no waffle grid inside |
| 315 | 8 | Cake or Omelet Baker Iron | same as waffle iron but no waffle grid inside |
| 343 | 3 | Utility Bowl with wood handle | |
| 401 | | Single Stove burner | |
| 434 | | 4 qt. Saucepan, cast aluminum | |
| 479 | 9 | Dutch Oven, not marked, patent 1920 | cover is p/n 482 |
| 506 | 8 | 5 quart Tea Kettle | |
| 635 | 5 | Victor Skillet | |
| 738 | 8 | Handled Griddle | |
| 768 | 8 | Cast Iron Chicken Pan, block TM with heat ring | |
| 768 | | Center Hinge Parts for early four-pan griddle | |
| 769 | | Square Fry Cover | for p/n 768 Square Fry Skillet |
| 769 | | Center Hinge Parts for early six-pan flop griddle | |
| 771 | 8 | Long Griddle | see p/n 745 |
| 820 | 8 | Bulge Pot with bail handle | |
| 837 | 8 | Dutch Oven Cover, earliest flat type | fits p/n 833 |
| 838 | 9 | Dutch Oven Cover, earliest flat type | fits p/n 834 |
| 839 | 4 | Scotch Bowl | |
| 851 | | Tea Kettle, flat bottom, size 7 | see p/n 846 |
| 856 | | Cover for Tea Kettle | fits p/n 847 |
| 861 | | Oval Tree Platter | |
| 866 | 8 | American Waffle Iron | |
| 875 | 7 | Erie Long Broiler | |
| 885 | | Wafer Iron | see p/n 860 |
| 889 | 8 | Waffle Iron, 1880, 93 patents | |
| 890 | 8 | Waffle Iron, 1880, 93 patents | |
| 908 | 8 | Long Griddle, late style, small TM | |
| 909 | 9 | Long Griddle, late style, small TM | |
| 921 | 7 | Oval Waffle Iron | frame p/n 916 |
| 922 | 7 | Oval waffle Iron | frame p/n 916 |
| 947 | | Lamb Cake Mold, early, large with legs out front | |
| 948 | | Lamb Cake Mold, early, large with legs out front | |
| 957 | 4 | Vienna Roll Pan, 4 cups | |
| 959 | 24 | Bread Pan, 6 cakes | |
| 960 | 26 | Bread Pan, 2 loaves | |
| 962 | | Munk Pan | |
| 977 | 8 | Same as other p/n 977 but "Griswold" and "New American" removed | |
| 981 | | Western Importing Co., Heart Shaped Waffle Iron similar to Andresen Iron | |
| 999 | | Western Importing Co., Heart Shaped Waffle Iron similar to Andresen Iron | |
| 1602 | | Coffee Pot – aluminum | |
| 1713 | | Coffee Pot | |
| 2106 | 6 | Skillet, hammered aluminum with wood handle | |
| 2106 | 8 | Skillet, hammered aluminum with wood handle | |

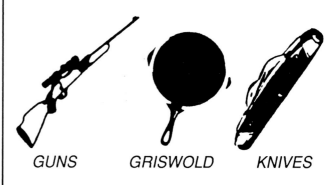